THE ART OF THE JAPANESE KITE

The

Art of the Japanese Kite

by
TAL STREETER

A SPECIAL EDITION PUBLISHED FOR
THE JAPAN SOCIETY, NEW YORK

New York · WEATHERHILL · *Tokyo*

The kite on the title page is a Sanjo rokkaku (hexagonal) kite portraying Oishi Yoshio, the famous leader of the Forty-seven Ronin. By Watanabe Toranosuke of Shirone, Niigata Prefecture.

Modern Japanese names in this book are given in the Western style (surname last), while premodern names follow the Japanese style (surname first).

First edition, 1974
Second printing, 1980

Published by John Weatherhill, Inc., of New York and Tokyo, with editorial offices at 7-6-13 Roppongi, Minato-ku, Tokyo 106, Japan. Protected by copyright under terms of the International Copyright Union; all rights reserved. Printed and first published in Japan.

LCC 74-76102   ISBN 0-8348-0157-4

to

Miho  father want him to

grow o

and

Kaku greatest classical

music qod

CONTENTS

Portfolio of Kites follows page 77

ACKNOWLEDGMENTS

I WISH TO GRATEFULLY ACKNOWLEDGE the help I received researching and writing this book. Particular thanks are due: Marty Davidson, who started me on the project by suggesting I write the book; Shoji Nakamura of the Shirone City Office; Ginko Hara, Chizuko Murakami, and Tatsuro Fukuda; David Kung, who visited and corresponded with Katsuta Yanase while gathering kites for New York City's Museum of Modern Art Children's Carnival; Akiko Saguchi of the Nagoya office and Warren Obluck of the Tokyo office of the U.S. Information Service; Takashi Nakamura and Haruo Kaminishizono of the Nagasaki City Tourist Section; Zen'ichi Koga of the Nagasaki Prefectural Tourist Office; Tatsuro Amagasaki, reporter for the *Nagasaki Shimbun;* Random House and author John Toland for permission to quote from *The Rising Sun;* Yusaku Tawara and Tadao Saito, authors of fine books on the Japanese kite; Misao Iijima and Mitsuko Hasegawa; the Shinzo Omura family and Seiichi and Heizo Ito of Hamamatsu; Tsutomu Hiroi, who suggested the chapter title "The Taste of Kites"; kite collector Shingo Modegi of the Taimeiken Restaurant, Tokyo; Makiko Onishi; the officers of the Hoshubana O-dako Association; and Sukey Hughes, who made some of the research materials for her own book on Japanese paper available to me. For much of the material in the concluding chapter on kite making and flying, which is based on articles that appeared in the American Kitefliers Association magazine *Kite Tales,* I would like to thank that association and its president, Robert M. Ingraham, who also kindly read through the chapter for accuracy.

To the Center for International Study, University of the State of New York; the administration of Bennett College, Millbrook, New York, who gave early impetus to my study of Japan; and Horace Smith, John Reynolds, Reiji Yamamoto, Toshiko Hara, Kosaku Fukawa, and Issac Shimizu, all of whom helped enlarge my experience and enjoyment of things uniquely Japanese, I give my thanks. I am particularly indebted to my friend Kuniyoshi Munakata, who traveled widely in Japan with me, introducing me to so many things I came to value including the books of his teacher, R. H. Blyth, whose haiku translation appears here through the courtesy of the Hokuseido Press, Tokyo, and Hallmark Cards, Inc.

Thanks are also due to my daughter Lissa, who assisted in interpreting and offered her own insights, as did my wife Dorothy Ann, whose enjoyment of the world has taken me to many places I would not otherwise have gone; and to Ronald V. Bell, Nina Raj, and Dana Levy, my editors and designer at John Weatherhill, Inc.

All photographs with the exception of those identified in caption credits are by the author, taken with Nikon equipment on Fujicolor and Fuji SS film with a small number on Kodachrome II and Kodak Tri-X film. Processing and printing in Japan was done by the laboratories of Cherry Camera Company, Shizuoka, and in the United States by the author with thanks to Peter Moore and the University of North Carolina-Greensboro for the use of their darkroom facilities.

THE ART OF THE JAPANESE KITE

PROLOGUE

THIS BOOK IS ABOUT KITES I have seen, kite makers I have spoken with, and kite festivals I have attended. The kites I make myself are quite large. The Japanese kites that most stir my imagination are even larger.

Japanese friends invariably introduce a kite-centered person like me as *tako-kichi,* "kite crazy." Introduced in this way, one hears many interesting stories about kites. Not surprisingly, such a novel subject provides a popular topic of conversation in Japanese bars. Recently, between free-flowing sakè and beer, I was asked if I had ever seen really small Japanese kites. I replied yes, about the size of postage stamps, adding that such kites were the hardest of all to fly. My bar friend said, "No, much smaller. Less than a quarter of an inch square, and flown with a line so fine that it is invisible to the human eye." He had seen them himself, he claimed, but didn't know in which district they were made.

Let me, then, add another dedication to this book: to a Japanese kite I have never seen and its maker, whom I have never met.

For one such as I, with an obsession for *o-dako,* or giant kites, a tiny, nearly invisible kite provides a fine balance. It also leaves this book unfinished—as it should be. The reader may yet discover this tiny kite for himself. Should he search with enough zeal, he may uncover even more fascinating and beautiful objects, traditions, and living people.

1

GIANT KITE FIGHTING IN SHIRONE

"THE TRAIN CAME OUT of the long tunnel into the snow country. The earth lay white under the night sky." So begins Nobel prize winner Yasunari Kawabata's *Snow Country*, a novel set in northwest Japan. Between December and April the railway tunnels of the Japanese alps are a signal of the approaching pleasures of skiing and hot spring resorts to fun seekers traveling from Tokyo by train, the only way into the area in winter.

For the farmers of the snow country, the hard winter is followed by a month of back-breaking work in which they must complete the spring planting before the rainy season begins. By early June, snow is visible only on the peaks of distant high mountains. Before the coming of the torrential rains of mid-June, the skies are clear blue and the winds blow lightly and pleasantly. Then, in a short respite from the arduous life of tilling the earth, the country people fly kites, turning their faces away from the harsh realities of the earth, up toward the freedom and release of a vaulting sky.

On a June day the Sado Express whisks me through the snow country, which is reflected in an upside-down world of flooded rice paddies. Late planting is still going on. Men, women, and children, the latter specially let out of school for the work, are standing shin-deep in flooded paddies. In deference to traditions of bygone times, when it was believed that a woman's fertility as the childbearer was transferred to the rice, the women do the actual planting, bent double at the waist as they transplant young green plants from special seed beds. They push the rice shoots down through the water, rooting them into the mud in neat rows with the stalks jutting six inches above the water's surface.

The farmers' houses stand low against the sky, their roofs covered with tiles of blue, green, and gray tones. The older farmhouses have thatch roofs, thick dark thatching that looks warm. Wide eaves keep snow and rain clear of the walls. Moss, grasses, and a gray lichen grow in pleasing irregular patterns on some of the thatch roofs, making the houses seem an outgrowth of the earth. The weather-stained unpainted walls blend almost imperceptibly into the earth, as though rooting the houses firmly and enduringly.

Our train leaves the mountains behind, and before us flooded rice paddies stretch ahead, receding out of sight toward the Japan Sea and the port city of Niigata. From there it is a short journey to my destination, Shirone city in Niigata Prefecture.

Shirone looks small, as though it could comfortably hold about two or three thousand people. The streets are narrow and long with few intersections, deceptively suggesting that there is nowhere else to go except straight on through the town, right back out into the surrounding farmland. Numerous small shops pushed against each other offer goods typical of a small country village, such as bamboo baskets and brooms. The one- and two-story buildings look very low after experiencing Tokyo's high-rise skyline. And though there are cars, people throng the streets as if automobiles didn't yet merit attention. You'd never guess it, but Shirone's population is 33,000.

Fifteen feet of accumulated winter snow has mercifully disappeared into the ground. The back-breaking labor of rice planting is just about over. And now, as during the second week of each June, the entire population turns itself loose for a *tako-kichi matsuri,* a kite-crazy festival, in which kites from rival teams fight in the sky.

During this festival week, red and white banners line all the store fronts. Schoolchildren playing wooden flutes parade the streets, and visiting firemen arrayed in rough formation behind big, slow-moving red fire engines march past a reviewing stand. In front of the shops are stacks of eight-foot-high fighting kites made in Shirone's traditional hexagonal shape. On them traditional kite designs in bright colors blend with advertising for the stores' goods. Several shops sell this kind of kite, called Sanjo *rokkaku,* smaller versions of the Sanjo district's hexagonal fighting kite, made by the three professional kite makers who live in the district. There are more kites and kite artifacts in Shirone city than I have ever seen before in one place. Pastry shops offer *o-sembei* crackers and *rakugan* sweets embossed with kite designs. Even *sasa dango,* for which the region is famous, is related to kites. This is a sweet bean-paste dumpling wrapped in three bamboo leaves tied with sedge. The bamboo leaves are peeled back and the bean paste eaten like a banana. Four or five of these sweets used to dangle from the Shirone kite flyer's sash, where they were handy for providing instant energy as he flew the big kites.

On the primary school grounds, a short walk from the canal where the kites are flown, flyers work on a giant kite, straightening the bridles—forty-two or forty-nine evenly spaced ropes arranged in vertical rows of six or seven each across the face of the kite. These are going to be braided into an easily manageable length before being carried to the festival flying area. Young children are skipping and dancing about. Old men run across the field, vigorously pulling a long line behind them, their eyes shining with pleasure. The happy faces, mine among them, reveal keen anticipation of the pleasure of seeing these big kites fly.

Inside a factorylike gymnasium building on the school grounds are great quantities of unbelievably large kites—twenty-two feet high by sixteen and a half feet wide—stacked flat on the floor, one on top of the other, in several long rows. At the other end of the cavernous room, teams of young men are repairing and making kites by pasting new paper to old bamboo frame "bones" (Plate 2). A young man, sitting in the middle of the big kite he is making, works with stacks of small sheets of locally made *washi*, handmade Japanese paper, fanning them out like a deck of cards. He dips a wide brush into a pan of wheat paste, applies the paste to the edges of a dozen sheets at once, then quickly joins them at their edges to form the single-sheet "skin" of the giant o-dako kite. Nearby, other men confer about the kite's design, then one chalks an outline on the large paper surface. Another swift hand boldly traces over the chalk lines with a large black-ink-loaded brush. Finally, the group working together fills in the outlines of the warriors, Kabuki-theater characters, legendary faces, carp, and butterflies, decorating with bright-colored dyes the kites that have flown in Shirone skies for several hundred years. As many as thirty each of a dozen different designs are made during festival time, for approximately that number quickly end up at the bottom of the canal waters over which they are flown—downed as quickly as they are made in this vast room.

The Shirone kites are flown all afternoon, from one to six, for seven days. In the morning the townspeople not working at the school grounds are all trading opinions on whether or not it will rain, how the wind will blow, and what the best flying techniques are, and discussing the weaknesses and strengths of rival teams. A cabdriver told me: "There are more reliably windy days in May, but then the rice must be planted." A camera store owner said that his father had a great interest in kites. He brought out a worn book in which his father had carefully recorded kite battles of fifty years ago. At the breakfast table we were told: "The wind is not strong enough today." But at lunch people agreed: "The wind is too strong." Across town a city employee at the newly constructed four-story city hall says, "The wind is blowing south now, but by this afternoon it will come from the north, the best wind for the Shirone kites." This man had participated in many kite festivals. The great majority of the men I met had flown kites in at least one of the past Shirone festivals. Behind all their comments and enthusiasm is a community history intricately and inextricably woven around kites.

From many stories I heard during my visit to Shirone, the following account emerged. Three hundred years ago the canal was built to take water to the ricefields. Kites were flown before then, of course, but the completion of the canal marked the beginning of the festival as it is now known. Gradually the canal was enlarged until it was wide enough to allow barges to carry provisions up and down its length. But one day, due to the canal's increased width, one bank became too weak and burst, flooding the eastern side, the village of Shirone. After repairing the damage, the feudal lord of Shibata County, a wise and wily former warrior named Mizoguchi, proposed that he give a prize for the best kites flown from the new canal bank—and the many sandaled feet that then ran over the fresh earth tamped it into a strong embankment.

Other popular accounts of the festival's origins do not necessarily dispute this story as much as suggest further developments in Shirone's long history of kite flying. Shibata County, on the east bank, was always the wealthier side of the canal, while Shirone Ajikata, on the west, was poor. The east bank villagers very often quarreled with the west bank farmers, and brawls involving many people were common. Lord Mizoguchi, it is said, suggested kite fighting as a substitute for street fighting.

Another story mentions that villagers' kites flown across the canal would often come tumbling down out of the sky, striking Shirone farmhouses with such force that tile or thatching was dislodged. Kites landing in rice paddies destroyed many plants. In anger, Shirone Ajikata farmers also took up kite flying and eventually kite fighting became a competition between the two towns. At that time, two hundred years ago, kites were half the size of the current giants. That, however, was large enough to do considerable damage—and the flying kites created a situation similar to that experienced today by people living at the edge of an airport, who are constantly frightened by the prospect of an object hurtling down at them out of the heavens.

Over the years many innovations and improvements have been made in the fighting capabilities of the Shirone kite. The rectangular giant kite, commonly called the o-dako, is twenty-two feet high by sixteen and a half feet wide (Plate 11). The other one is the newer eight-foot-high hexagonal three-bone kite, a hundred years old in design and referred to as the Sanjo rokkaku (Plates 10, 19). This hexagonal kite is unusual and quite practical in design in that removal of the center bone allows the kite to be rolled up and easily carried—a problem with giant kites, which can only be rolled loosely into a large tube (Plate 3). Formerly this kite had two diagonal vertical bones. I was told that the diagonal bones made it easier to fly, but weakened its fighting capabilities. Other improvements that have been made on these two kinds of kites are less apparent to the eye. The east and west bank kites have distinctive and subtle features equally difficult to discern: The west side's giant rectangular kites, for example, have heavier horizontal bamboo bones at the top that become progressively narrower in size and light in weight toward the bottom. This allows the kite to rise quickly and to make sudden swooping dives from above. The east side o-dako are heavier at the bottom and their bridle ropes are shorter on the right, allowing them to move swiftly to the right. Since the object of the battles at Shirone is to bring the other side's kite crashing down into the water, each side's kite is designed with long-established knowledge of the wind's habits in relation to their side of the canal as well as to the peculiarities of their opponent's kites and flying techniques.

Both the rectangular giant kite and the smaller hexagonal Sanjo rokkaku are kenka-dako, warring or fighting kites. The "peaceful fighting" that Lord Mizoguchi originally instituted is practiced now by four teams on the west side and eight teams on the east. Each team consists of from four to twelve members. The smaller kites require four or five men to fly them; the larger kites, from eight to twelve.

By noon on kite-fighting days a huge crowd lines the Nakanokuchi Canal, waiting impatiently for the kite fighting to begin. Most of the crowd wanders up and down the canal banks, crossing back and forth to the east and west sides over bridges about a half-mile from either end of what will soon be the center of activity. People walk together in small groups, calling to friends and stopping to discuss the merits of their own teams and to second-guess the wind and weather. Families sit together protected from the sun beneath awnings erected at the top of each side of the canal bank. Sometimes there are as many as three or four generations together.

Soon, down the main street, coming toward the canal, run two kite flyers, one in front of the other. They carry on their shoulders a thick bamboo pole over which is loosely draped a very heavy kite rope. Rumbling slowly behind them is a bright yellow city dump truck that today carries a kite rolled up loosely in the shape of a giant tube. The kite takes up the whole bed of the truck, with a quarter of its length hanging out over the open tailgate. At the canal flying area, the truck is met by a team of flyers. They lift the kite out, then run with it up a dirt path to the canal bank, three or four men on each side and several underneath holding it above their heads.

A light wind blows from somewhere gently rustling the hair and clothes of the watchers on both sides of the canal. One group of onlookers cheers the approaching team and their giant kite, while another part of the crowd farther down the canal grows silent as they watch the first kite, a rokkaku, streak into the sky from the east and hang low in insolent challenge to the men of the west bank (Plates 17, 18). The team members pause to catch their breath, wiping sweat from their foreheads with the loose kerchiefs that hang about their necks. Suddenly a challenger shoots into the air from the opposite bank. Within minutes the sky is crowded with fighting kites racing upward, diving and cutting across one another's paths. Two of the kite lines tangle, then two more. All along the canal the kite lines are crisscrossing one another. In the midst of the confusing mass, one kite falters, seeming to lose its balance, then erratically tumbles down out of the sky. Its east bank attacker follows it down more smoothly, though the two lines are snared together. A second before the attacked kite touches the canal water its team pulls suddenly on their line in an attempt to wrench the east bank kite out of the sky and over to their side of the canal. Before they can do this, the east bank team calls for help and twenty-five or thirty of their friends and neighbors rush out of the watching crowd to grab the kite line—actually a strong rope—and pull for all they are worth in a tug of war to determine the final victor.

The two mangled kites hang suspended midway out over the water, their bridles ensnarled, their flying lines stretched taut to either side of the canal. And the fighting is still on. The west bank team, now also joined by men, women, and children of all ages, is laughing and pulling with great vigor. They run with three or four hundred feet of line back down the outside of the canal bank, then down an incredibly steep sloping ramp that is precariously balanced on telephone poles, and race across the railroad tracks on the western side (Plate 16). But then their kite line breaks unexpectedly, and the tug-of-war volunteers fall back on each other like a collapsing row of dominoes. Amid shouts of victory, the broken line is immediately pulled to the east bank of the canal. While the winners wave the broken kite over their heads in a victory salute, the losing team begins preparing another kite for flying, for they may fly as many as a dozen kites in one day of the festival if their luck doesn't improve. There are anywhere from thirty to fifty of the hexagonal rokkaku kites flying throughout the afternoon (Plate 1). Kites soar up and plummet down. Men scramble up tiled roofs to relaunch a fallen kite from the peak. No one person can take in the whole spectacle, there is so much of it. And what has just been described has taken no more than twenty minutes. The afternoon has just begun, and we have yet to see the giant kites flying!

At the lower bridge of the canal the giant kite has been made ready for flying. To help it fly, it is laid out flat on the ground, face down, then bowed back and tied with lines from side to side to curve its face. The flyers all wear *happi* coats emblazoned with their team's emblem, which also ornaments their kite (Plates 4–7). Ten men position themselves along each of the kite's long sides and lift it slightly off the ground. Several others straighten out the bridles and flying line that lie on the canal path ahead of the kite for a distance of about a hundred feet. A dozen team members clear an aisle through the crowd for themselves and the kite line. They station themselves along one side of the rope, holding it loosely, awaiting the signal to run forward. Then, at the signal, the team members brace themselves and charge forward, straining with the weight and sudden effort of pulling the kite against the light wind. Those holding the kite itself run a short distance with the kite's top edge held slightly higher than the back, letting go when the kite lifts up into the wind.

The mammoth kite moves ever so slowly down the path behind the flyers, still more horizontal than vertical, just barely missing the heads of watchers, some of whom duck down in fright as the monster momentarily blocks out the sun. Its long rope tail swishes languidly through the crowd, which has become silent, the people clenching their teeth and straining as though to lift the kite with concentrated willpower. Slowly, very slowly, the giant kite moves out over the water, its face rising into the wind. For a while, though it is flying, it does not gain altitude. Its tail skims the water, rippling the surface. The crowd watches the falling kite silently. But then the kite slowly begins to rise into the sky, where it is finally caught and held by the wind at a height of about five hundred feet. A roar of approval goes up to it from the watchers. Three-quarters of a mile down the canal path some of the flyers drop to the ground exhausted. Others immediately take their place, straining to keep the kite line from pulling through their fingers.

Viewers are allowed to contemplate this beautiful sight for only a few minutes, for on the other bank the opposing kite is being readied. It moves in slow motion out over the water and seems to hover there, its tail skimming the surface. It slowly lifts, then dips again, and finally is allowed to drop gently onto the grassy slope of the canal bank for lack of wind to hold it aloft. The team tries again: the kite's tail skims along the water and starts to lift, but then one corner touches the water and the kite suddenly knifes downward, sinking quickly out of sight. A sigh goes up from the watchers as the water is stained by the brightly colored dyes—the red, blue, yellow, orange, and purple that shortly before had been a beautiful painting of a samurai. Then the bare bones erupt from the water and are pulled out, to be used again in next year's festival (Plates 12–15). Other attempts are made to launch another giant kite, but these too fail, and for a while at least, the single giant which flies among the smaller rokkaku kites is safe from attack.

About an hour has passed since the first kite appeared. The sight of the Shirone kites hanging in the afternoon sky is indescribably beautiful. Their combat is exciting and their death in the canal poignant. For me, and for many others, the festival need not ever end.

2

THE SANJO KITE MAKER
TORANOSUKE WATANABE

A FAIR WAS BEING HELD at the Shirone temple grounds, and on the second day of the festival we paid it a visit. Among the booths offering food, games, and novelties we unexpectedly came upon a stall filled with Shirone kites. There, surrounded by masses of richly colored kites, an old man with a red and white cloth band tied rakishly around his forehead caught our eye with the vigor of his gestures. He had that crinkled, cheerful face and spontaneous gaiety that bring to mind Santa Claus, happy old grandfathers in children's stories, or a minor character in a Charles Dickens' novel. He really twinkled! I supposed that he must be the Shirone kite maker—nothing less! It wasn't long, however, before I relearned the old adage about appearances being deceiving. While I was taking pictures of "my Shirone kite maker," a nondescript, fiftyish-looking man wearing ordinary plastic-framed eyeglasses, a gray jacket, and an open-necked sports shirt introduced himself to me. He was, he said, Toranosuke Watanabe, the Shirone kite maker (Plate 26).

So much for the fictions we borrow from fairy tales and films. Like most Japanese kite makers, Watanabe does not look as he might be expected to. That naturally did not stop us from accepting his invitation to visit his home and talk about Sanjo kites.

We followed him through the quiet streets. Now, with nearly everyone at the canal, most of the shops were closed. Earlier in the day the hexagonal rokkaku fighting kites had been displayed in front of these shops, but now there were no kites to be seen. We had thought they were advertising kites because each one had the shop name worked into the traditional Sanjo shape. Then it became clear: the kites had been carried to the canal to be used in the aerial combat—Kodak Camera from the middle of the block battled Toshiba Electric from the shop down the street.

Watanabe's workshop and home also contained a toy shop. Inside, the place was crowded with tables stacked high with kites and a variety of toys. We followed the kite maker into the cluttered combination workshop-living room at the rear of the store, where, incidentally, he turns out 5,000 kites each year. It took little prodding to get him to talk about kites and kite making. "The big rectangular Shirone kites, the o-dako, and the hexagonal rokkaku kites, both of which are used for fighting, are not made by professional kite makers but by men from other trades who have varying degrees of skill in bamboo work and drawing. The bamboo bones of their kites are strong, so that only a few of the bones are destroyed in kite battles. The unbroken bones are saved from year to year and thus the bones may be quite old.

"The men who make the bamboo bones are not professional kite makers. But bamboo craftsmanship is not the special province of the kite maker. In rural Shirone, bamboo, as well as paper, is still a part of everyday life for many people. The special knowledge required for making the big kites is passed along from generation to generation. The kite maker's ability is a special one, but the big kites they make are not particularly refined. They don't have to be; so many are flown in a festival that expediency is as important as art. The kites must be very strong. This consideration introduces an element of roughness into their appearance. They have a certain beauty, however, the crude beauty of the straightforward utilitarian and perishable object whose life is actually quite brief.

"The men who make these festival kites are kite makers by avocation. It is a once-a-year activity for them, a short respite from their daily labors. My kites are very different. For me there are only kites, all year long, year after year."

Watanabe's kites come in a variety of sizes (Plates 37–39, 57). Most of them, two to three feet in height, are smaller than the festival kites. He does, however, take special orders and make kites as large as the festival rokkaku kite. Tokyo's paper museum at Horifune in Kita Ward has a large kite made by Watanabe, and its samurai painting is considerably more skillful than those of the festival kites that end their lives so quickly in the waters of the canal. His Sanjo kite is made only in the hexagonal rokkaku shape, whereas the rectangular o-dako shape made by the once-a-year kite maker is used only for the annual festival.

Watanabe's kites are not flown in the festival at all, but many are sold to visitors and local people at festival time. Throughout the year and particularly at New Year's and on May fifth (Boys' Day, now called Children's Day), when kites are traditionally flown, the Sanjo rokkaku will be found on sale in department stores and shops across Japan.

The Watanabe family did not invent the Sanjo kite nor are they its sole maker. There are two other Sanjo rokkaku kite makers in Niigata Prefecture. Watanabe belongs to a group of professional kite makers whose members, scattered throughout Japan, number about 130. Most of these men—there is one Japanese woman currently making kites—make kites as a full-time profession. Some supplement the generally meager income derived from kite making with money earned from a second job. Yanase, the Yokosuka kite maker, for example, makes lanterns as well as kites.

Kite making is a family tradition that is passed on from father to eldest son. In former times there was virtually no alternative open to an eldest son other than that of carrying on his father's business or profession. If the son did not continue in his father's footsteps, which was quite rare, or if there were no son, it was common and quite acceptable for the family to adopt one. The special skills necessary for Japan's unique arts were often maintained by virtue of this practice of adoption. Faced with the necessity of an adoption, the family took great pains to find a young person who showed promise of marked talent for the profession into which he would be apprenticed.

Toranosuke Watanabe explained that he is the fifth generation of the Watanabe family to make kites. He had spent three years studying traditional woodblock printing before he was officially adopted by and apprenticed to his uncle Sukegoro. His enthusiasm and talent for drawing convinced his uncle that he would do well as a kite maker. Toranosuke accepted— it may have been difficult to refuse once the family had agreed that it was a wise course— thus ensuring the continuation of kite making in the Watanabe family for another generation.

Such decisions are not easily reached. A kite maker's life is not an exciting one; in fact it is rarely free of monotony. There is some variety in drawing kite designs, but kite making is largely a repetitive occupation. If Watanabe is to make 5,000 kites a year, he must complete about seventeen kites a day. If there is little variety in the work, still less invention is required; the kite maker does not generally deviate from well-established patterns.

On the positive side, there is the considerable satisfaction the kite maker may derive from the knowledge that he is working in virtually the exact manner of his predecessor. More than likely, he will sit in the same spot that his forefathers did and hold tools whose wooden handles have been worn smooth. There is great pleasure to be had in close affinity with the past, although it is not one that enjoys much recognition in modern times.

In Japan, respect for one's ancestors and traditional practices reflect a clear realization of how things of value are preserved through the passing of time. Neither death nor violent typhoons or earthquakes are allowed to create chaos. Continuity within change is primary. The kite string of the modern kite artist is held by his ancestors as well as by his young successor. The simple, uncluttered art of the kite serves well, in the midst of a rapidly changing society of transistors, computers, and nuclear reactors, to anchor Japan to the past. It is characteristic of the Japanese that they preserve the best of the past while striding energetically into the future.

I asked Watanabe what he considered the principal element of kite making. "Not drawing the picture, as you might guess," he replied. "That is secondary. I wish to make kites that the owner can fly as freely as he wishes—as if the kite itself has life! That is of the greatest importance to me."

The kite maker's friend, who had joined us, mentioned that Watanabe was a splendid kite flyer. "He makes his kites turn twenty times to the right and twenty times to the left, then brings them down to skim the canal's water," he said with admiration.

We had talked through the late afternoon into early evening. Before leaving, I purchased many of Watanabe's Sanjo rokkaku kites. As he tied the bridle strings to my selections, he explained that although the dyes used for kites were customarily bright, he himself preferred more subdued colors. Wrapping my kites in a piece of paper, he added a gift of a kite drawing of a samurai. "It is identical," he said, "to the one chosen by the prefectural government and presented as a gift to the emperor." He was quite proud of this "good drawing." The picture had been rendered in the subdued colors of *doro enogu,* a kind of opaque pigment considered the material of refined artists, instead of in the customary brightly colored kite dyes.

As a last question, I asked him which was his favorite Japanese kite. Other kite makers had modestly declined to answer this question. After all, they had devoted their lives to their own kites and could hardly answer honestly other than to choose one of their own designs. Toranosuke Watanabe, however, answered without hesitation, "I prefer the Nagasaki kite over all others. It has beautiful, simple color combinations, is wonderfully made, and is an unparalleled fighter."

On that note we returned to our inn, where we enjoyed a dinner of fresh vegetable delicacies and a kind of meat stew that was perhaps invented on the spot for American tastes. For dessert we were served a bowl heaped full of big, sweet, magnificently formed strawberries that had been dipped in powdered sugar. And at last we slept, on soft *futon* mattresses laid on tatami, dreaming of kites that had been and would be again, hopefully forever.

1. Four hexagonal kites being maneuvered into strategic positions at the Shirone kite-fighting festival. ▷

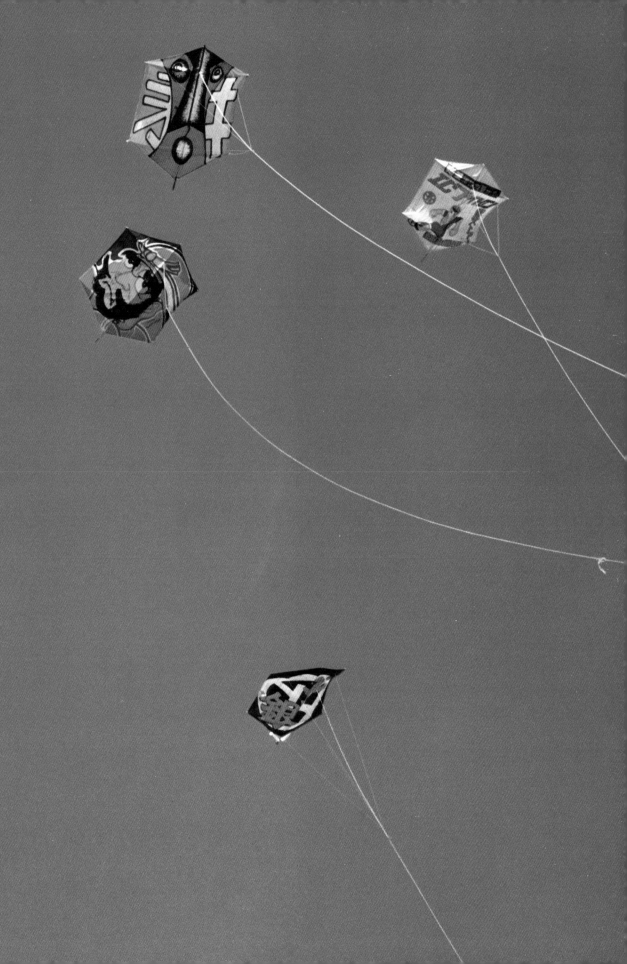

2. Shirone kite makers taking a break among the giant o-dako kites they have painted in the school gymnasium. Shirone, Niigata Prefecture.

3. (opposite) O-dako, giant kites, are loosely folded or rolled into large tubes and carried through the streets from the school to the fighting area. Shirone, Niigata Prefecture.

4–7. The happi coats worn by the flyers bear their team's insignia, often the same colorful and distinctive one that adorns the kites they fly. Shirone, Niigata Prefecture.

8. The bridle and flying lines of a fighting kite at the annual kite-fighting festival. Shirone, Niigata Prefecture.

9. Tying the crossbones on a Sanjo rokkaku. This three-bone kite has one vertical bone; when this is removed, the 8-foot-high kite can be rolled up and conveniently carried. Shirone, Niigata Prefecture.

10. The hexagonal fighting kites also double as advertising banners for shops and business groups. Shirone, Niigata Prefecture.

11. (opposite) When it is aloft, this giant kite is a challenge to giant kites from the other side of the canal. Here the intricate pattern of the bridle lines adds to the kite's beauty. These rectangular kites are about 22 by 16 1/2 feet and require from eight to twelve men to fly them. Shirone, Niigata Prefecture.

16. With two fighting kites mangled, bridle lines ensnarled, and lines stretched taut to either side of the canal, en- ▷
thusiastic friends help pull the rope to determine the final victor. Here they are several hundred feet from the fighting
area, pulling the flying line across railway lines. Courtesy of Shirone Municipal Sightseeing Department.

12–15. The warrior of this downed kite appears aghast at the prospect of the dunking he is about to get. As soon as the
kite becomes wet, the paper begins to deteriorate. For a brief moment, the beautiful pigments of the design lend the
water their bright hues; then only the strings and bare bones remain, later to be pulled out and used in next year's competition. Shirone, Niigata Prefecture.

17. A Sanjo rokkaku going up to take part in a kite fight. It takes a team of about four or five men to handle a kite of this size. Shirone, Niigata Prefecture.

18. (above, right) A beautiful kite like this is not allowed to fly for very long. In a short while another hexagonal kite will engage it in a darting, crisscrossing battle that will end with the two kites falling toward the canal with their flying lines entangled. Shirone, Niigata Prefecture.

19. (right) A Sanjo rokkaku kite with a warrior design and an advertisement for a local architectural firm. The hexagonal kite is about 8 feet high, and its design a hundred years old. Shirone, Niigata Prefecture.

20. (opposite) In a cluttered workshop, the Yokosuka kite maker Matsutaro Yanase works on a colorful monkey showman, or *saru mawashi*, kite. See Plates 34–35, 49–51, 53, 84, 86 for other Yanase kites.

26. The Sanjo kite maker Toranosuke Watanabe sitting by his hexagonal rokkaku kites in his workshop. Shirone, Niigata Prefecture. See Plates 37–39, 57 for other Watanabe kites.

21. The Edo kite maker's wife wrapping kite bones with thin strips of paper. The paper face of the kite is more readily glued to bamboo bones wrapped in this fashion. Tokyo.

22–25. (below) Edo kite maker Teizo Hashimoto painting one of his warrior kites. The first drawing is done lightly in charcoal, and he later goes over it in dark *sumi* ink. See Plate 41 for completed kite; see also Plates 40, 42, 43, 48, 85 for other Hashimoto kites.

27. The sophisticated reel that is used by Hamamatsu teams to rapidly let out and retrieve line in order to gain the advantage of maneuverability. Hamamatsu, Shizuoka Prefecture.

30. Each year on the emperor's birthday, April 29, ▷ the sky above Nagasaki's Mount Tohakkei is filled with warring hata kites participating in the *hata-age,* or hata kite-fighting contest. Courtesy of Nagasaki Prefectural Tourist Office.

28–29. Hamamatsu kite flyers in their distinctive uniforms, happi coats decorated with their team emblems. The same emblems appear on the teams' kites. Hamamatsu, Shizuoka Prefecture.

31. Suruga kite maker Tatsusaburo Kato at work. See Plates 44–47 for other Kato kites. Shizuoka. Courtesy of *Asahi Shimbun*.

32. Juta Yanase (right), the samurai turned kite maker, with his wife and their grandson Matsutaro in a photograph taken in 1920.

34–35. Front and back views of a beka kite portraying two mythical creatures who appear ready to lock tooth and fang in deadly battle. The back view of the kite shows the arrangement of the bones. By Matsutaro Yanase, Yokosuka, Shizuoka Prefecture.

33. Insect kite maker Semmatsu Iwase. See Plates 63, 67, 68 for Iwase kites. Sakurai, Aichi Prefecture.

3

THE LAST KITE MAKER OF TOKYO:
EDO KITE MAKER TEIZO HASHIMOTO

AT THE HEIGHT of the kite's popularity in Japan, in the middle of the eighteenth century, there were approximately one hundred kite makers in Edo, now called Tokyo. As late as World War II there were thirty-five. Since then the tall buildings and new diversions of this modern city have further reduced the number of Tokyo's kite makers to only one, Teizo Hashimoto.

The broad thoroughfare leading from Ueno Station, Tokyo's second largest train station, toward the southern Ueno district is lined with large shops selling the religious objects used in Buddhist temples and private home altars. Branching off the main thoroughfare are many narrow, erratically tangled streets of shops. Though some of Tokyo's buildings are taller and the main avenues wider, the side streets of the world's largest city are not unlike those of a small city such as Shirone. The shops huddle close together, hardly distinguishable from one another. Most of them have sliding glass doors that extend across the front and open directly onto the shop; the living quarters for the shop owner and his family are usually located directly behind or above the shops.

Outside a bow-and-arrow maker's shop stand bundles of thin, straight bamboo. Inside, two craftsmen are at work making arrows. One man quickly heats a long, thin bamboo stalk over a small ceramic stove. He then sights along its length and straightens it with a simple wooden tool while it is still warm. The other craftsman pares and trims the nodes to make the perfect cylindrical form of a slender arrow, then completes the work by adding the tip, nock,

◁ 36. Flyers and a large kite at the Hamamatsu kite festival.

and feathers. Long, narrow, laminated bamboo bows stand upright in neat rows against the wall. These bows are used by archery students as well as Zen Buddhist priests who seek to develop a harmonious body and mind through the discipline of archery.

Here in south Ueno, as is true throughout Tokyo and all of Japan, the rich and the poor often live next door to one another in the same neighborhood. Across the street from modern buildings that house the corporate offices of international concerns are to be found tiny old shops selling everyday necessities and some of the small pleasures of daily life.

To a stranger's eyes—almost everyone is a stranger, including the Tokyoite outside his own neighborhood—much of Tokyo is a confusing jumble. As there are few street names, it is invariably difficult to find a place the first time. A cabdriver has the same difficulty, but he eventually gets his passengers to their destination by stopping frequently to ask directions.

ON THE DAY of my visit to Hashimoto's shop I had chosen to walk and was enjoying the many discoveries it is possible to make while walking in Tokyo. I nearly missed Hashimoto's house, a little place squeezed between the other buildings on a long block, several corners beyond the bow-and-arrow maker's shop.

There was no sign hanging in front, but taped to the glass of the sliding entry doors were two small *tako-e,* kite paintings without bamboo bones. One of these was his beautiful painting of an ocean wave (Plate 40). Inside the entryway, surrounded by the clutter that is perhaps typical of all kite makers' shops, were many kites of varied sizes in different stages of completion; a barking dog and a playful kitten romped over the kites piled on the floor. I was greeted by a friend of the Hashimotos who was to act as interpreter. Hashimoto and his wife, seated on the floor, were both industriously working on Edo kites. Above their heads, near the ceiling, were bamboo poles crossing from wall to wall, and resting on these poles were stacks of kites. The angry-looking black eyes of the Indian Zen sage Daruma (Bodhidharma, Plate 43) glared down on the work below.

Beneath the Daruma kite the Hashimotos continued their work, pausing only to respond to my questions, their eyes and fingers busy at making kites. The brows of both Hashimotos are set in a permanent wrinkle at the nose from the long hours of concentration on the delicate work. As we talked, Mrs. Hashimoto patiently wrapped strip after strip of narrow paper diagonally along the length of the bamboo bones (Plate 21). She explained that there is a slight improvement in the bond between these paper-wrapped bones and the kite's paper skin, as paste does not stick to bamboo well. Wrapping the bones this way is commonly recognized as the mark of a high-quality kite. If there was any boredom in this interminably repetitive work, it was not reflected on her face or in her easy laugh. "I enjoy helping my husband make kites," she assured us very early in the conversation. Her pride and pleasure in the Edo kite are due in part perhaps to the fact that her father Tomekichi Hashimoto, who died three years ago at the age of eighty-eight, was the previous Edo kite maker. Teizo had apprenticed himself to the older man at the age of thirteen, later married Tomekichi's daughter and, according to traditional practice, carried on his father-in-law's business and had assumed his name as well as.

The best-known Edo kite design is an elaborate and detailed painting of a warrior or warriors in armor (Plate 42). This kite painting is called *nishiki-e,* or brocade picture, a reference to the painting style derived from the Edo *ukiyo-e* woodblock pictures of the mid-eighteenth century. Teizo Hashimoto is a master of this style of kite drawing. He does not, however, limit himself to this particular type of design and produces a variety of kites (Plates 41, 48, 85), all of which bring higher than average prices in recognition of the skill with which they are made and their importance as Edo kites. It was the Edo ukiyo-e and this type of kite, with its two hundred years of tradition, that has most strongly influenced the kites made throughout Japan today.

In the shop entryway, awaiting the addition of colored dyes and bamboo bones, were many elaborate black-ink drawings on handmade paper that had been draped over bamboo poles. There were even larger quantities of woodblock-printed drawings ready for coloring. Hashimoto has modernized his kite making, as have many kite makers, with the simple expedient of using woodblocks to print a black outline. Before, the outlines of the kite picture were done with brush and *sumi* (India) ink. The new method reduces some of the unique hand-made qualities of the kite, but the brilliant colors are still applied by hand. Most kite artists still draw and paint entirely with brush. Kites made commercially by silk-screen and offset printing processes are not in the same class at all. Because the Edo kite has patterns that are so complicated, colors that are so rich and varied, and very clear outlines, it is sometimes difficult to tell the completely hand-painted kite from that having the woodblock-printed outline. Woodblock printing allows Hashimoto to produce ten kites a day, whereas if he did them completely by hand he could make only four or five. I wondered if, as a consequence of this modernization, he still retained his facility for drawing the complex *sumi* ink pictures.

At my request, Hashimoto began a painting of one of his popular warriors in armor (Plates 22–25). This one was done entirely by hand. He made the first drawing very lightly in charcoal. With this sketchy outline completed, he poured a small amount of water from a metal teakettle into a shallow inkstone. Then he took a stick of *sumi* ink and rubbed it on the sloping edge of the inkstone, mixing the dry ink with water until he got the color and consistency he required. At first there was some nervousness and hesitancy. His hands shook, so he balanced his right hand on the left and flourished the brush above the paper, drawing in the air as a kind of warming-up exercise. After a minute of this, his arm moved downward and the brush touched paper: first he painted the nose, then the outline of the eyes, followed by the many details that make up this elaborately detailed painting.

The picture Hashimoto drew was a fine blend of delicate and bold lines, broad sweeping curves and tiny arcs, and light accents in a strong overall design. His hand, seeming to grow more steady as he forgot the circle of intently watching strangers, took on a rhythm, almost mechanical (yet at the same time like unself-conscious dancing), that produced of its own accord a beautiful drawing. One of the last elements he drew was a perfect freehand circle—surely a strain for him as it is for even those Zen priests who practice drawing circles with one dramatic swoop of inner and outward harmony. Unlike those drawn by Zen monks, Hashimoto's inward and outward harmony was expressed in a circle made with two strokes.

Nearing the completion of his drawing, he chose a flat, wide brush and painted the broad mustache and hair of the soldier. Traditionally a drawing is not considered to have life until the pupils of the eyes are added; Hashimoto finished the drawing with these life-giving dots. The black-ink drawing took him about ten minutes to complete—the most recent ten minutes of a tradition several hundred years old. He himself, Hashimoto told me, has produced perhaps a million of these hand-drawn pictures.

SOMETIME AFTER OUR MEETING, I learned that another Edo kite maker had recently died. This man, Takizo Hayashi, had been designated by the government as a Living National Treasure, the highest appellation conferred on outstanding artists working in the traditional arts. I was told by a member of the Tokyo National Research Institute of Cultural Properties, the government agency responsible for making recommendations, that the honor had yet to be passed on to another kite maker.

Teizo Hashimoto is now sixty-seven. He has no sons and no successor. Where there were once a hundred Edo kite makers, now there is only one.

4

ALONG THE TOKAIDO ROAD:
SURUGA KITE MAKER TATSUSABURO KATO

LOOKING NORTH TOWARD TOKYO from the paths of Nihon Daira mountain near my home, Mount Fuji can be seen high against the sky. Its southern slope is a long, softly curving line that rises gently off the ground—almost from sea level—and with gathering speed soars suddenly upward to the volcanic rim over twelve thousand feet above. Usually wreathed in clouds, it often pokes its summit through them by mid-morning. Sometimes while walking those paths thirty miles to the south of Mount Fuji, I would look up expecting to see that beautiful mountain. After a moment of bewildered searching, I would find it, looming far higher above me than I had expected, all but its magnificent summit blotted out by clouds.

Our house, lying in the prime tea-growing region of Japan, is surrounded by long rows of deep green tea bushes. To the east, beyond the sharp tops of pines and cedars and groves of tall, thin bamboo, are flat cutouts of mountains silhouetted in shades of gray. In the haze, the mountains are grainy looking, like overenlarged photographs. With the coming of the evening sun, the moisture-laden air takes on a pink tinge. To the west is the blue Pacific; to the south, on a black sand beach, the waters of Suruga Bay roll quietly; and at the center sprawls the modern city of Shizuoka, the home of Tatsusaburo Kato.

Perhaps it is not too much of an exaggeration to say that a great many of the views Westerners have of the landscape and people of Japan are based on that country's colorful ukiyo-e (literally, "pictures of the floating world"). These prints have been collected and prized by museums and connoisseurs throughout the world since the late nineteenth century (just as their popularity in Japan was declining). Ukiyo-e originated in Japan in the late seventeenth century as a popular art depicting genre scenes. These portrayals of Kabuki actors and the pleasure quarters, real and imagined landscapes, the everyday life of the people, and the exploits of legendary figures were extremely successful almost from their first appearance.

About two hundred years ago the ukiyo-e style of painting became the basis for many of the Japanese kite pictures. Tatsusaburo Kato's kites are drawn in this style. Appropriately enough, he lives in an area familiar to many who, though they have never been to Japan, recognize it from Ando Hiroshige's famous series of ukiyo-e landscape prints, *Fifty-three Stations of the Tokaido Road*. Shizuoka city at the time Hiroshige's prints were made was known as Fuchu. A short distance to the south, down the Tokaido Road, is Yokosuka (in Shizuoka Prefecture), which lies between the two old Tokaido stations, Kakegawa and Fukuroi. Several stops farther down is Hamamatsu; farther still, Okazaki. These names have remained unchanged and can be found on contemporary maps.

The scenes from Hiroshige's series were drawn at or near the government relay stations and inns built along the road between Edo and Kyoto. It was at these stations that foot-weary travelers journeying between the cities of Edo (where the headquarters of the shogun, the actual ruler of Japan, was situated) and Kyoto (where the emperor resided), changed horses and rested for the night. The year 1832, when Hiroshige first sketched his prints of the Tokaido, is far in the past, but today sections of the old road may still be found, if not imagined, as one travels the hundred miles from Tokyo south to Suruga Bay.

Today there is a superexpressway, the Tomei Highway, which sometimes touches the path of the old Tokaido, as does the older Highway One, which is still a main traffic artery. The streamlined, blue and white Shinkan Line "bullet trains" move passengers along the route of the old Tokaido from Tokyo through Kyoto and on to Osaka in air-conditioned comfort at a speed of 120 miles an hour. For those slightly adventurous travelers who wish to recapture a little of the past, however, it is still possible to stroll along between the gnarled pines that line the sides of the surviving stretches of the Tokaido. And the scenery of hundreds of years ago—the old trees, the relatively unchanged mountains against the sky, and the ocean surf beating against the black sand beaches—so stirs the imagination that it is almost possible to hear the processions of richly clad noblemen riding in palanquins borne on the shoulders of sweating bearers chanting the rhythmic heave-ho shout, "Yoi-sho, yoi-sho, yoi-sho!"

Long ago, in the early 1500s, nearly three hundred years before Hiroshige immortalized the towns and other scenic spots along the Tokaido, the lord of Suruga Castle, Imagawa Yoshimoto, had one of his retainers fly a kite over the castle walls as a sign of victory in a minor skirmish. This use of a kite marked the beginning of the Suruga kite. But the Imagawas did not have too many more opportunities to fly kites; in 1569 the head of the Takeda clan took over as the coastal chieftain. And in the early 1600s, after centuries of civil strife, Japan was unified under one feudal lord, Tokugawa Ieyasu. With the Tokugawa clan's supremacy secure throughout Japan, fighting between the daimyos (feudal lords) ended. The Suruga kite, first flown as a signal of victory in battle, remained as a colorful element of peaceful holiday celebrations.

Kites are customarily flown on May fifth (Boys' Day) and at New Year's. One can still see the Suruga kite—rectangular at the top and pointed at the bottom so that it looks a little like a wide arrow pointing downward—flying high above Shizuoka's tea fields and rice paddies, and above the broad Abe River, the traditional kite-flying area, that flows by the southwest edge of the city.

Modern Shizuoka city, with a population of 450,000, has many tall buildings and branches of all the major department stores. The city is in every way modern. Cosmopolitan Tokyoites, however, still retain the image of Shizuoka as it is presented in Hiroshige's drawings, a provincial farming community known primarily for its oranges and tea.

Although the citizens of Shizuoka consider themselves quite modern, the Suruga kite maker, Tatsusaburo Kato (Plate 31), holds views of Shizuoka that are closer to those of Tokyoites. For many Shizuokans, Kato is a bit of an anachronism from feudal times; he is admired for his art and honored by cultural heritage commissions, but remains a shadow of the past rather than a living person participating in the present.

Kato's grandfather, Hachizo, managed an inn. His great-grandfather was a samurai. Kato recalls that his grandfather continued to wear his hair in the samurai style—shaved in the middle, bound in the back with a long narrow band, and folded over toward the forehead in a topknot—long after most warriors had given up this status symbol. He also clung to the title "samurai," which had been dropped after the Meiji Restoration, the event that brought down the Tokugawa government in 1868. A good kite artist, Hachizo was known as a talented amateur, perhaps even a semiprofessional. Near the end of the Meiji era, at the turn of the nineteenth century, Tokujiro, Hachizo's son, opened a kite workshop in Suruga beneath a sign reading "Tako Hachi." The same sign still hangs over the door of the present shop. It's message is a play on words: tako or kite also means "octopus" and hachi means "eight," referring to the eight legs of an octopus. Taken together the words are an allusion to an earlier period when kites were often made in the shape of an octopus, its legs the kite's tails.

The present Suruga kite maker, Tatsusaburo Kato, started his apprenticeship under his father when he was sixteen years old. His father had a repertoire of sixty warrior and Kabuki actor faces that he drew on his kites in ukiyo-e style. His son, who had always taken his profession seriously, has doubled that number through diligent reading of history. As a young man he frequently attended Kabuki performances, where he studied the actors' makeup and facial expressions.

The Suruga kite of today (Plates 44, 46) resembles those made when Tako Hachi first opened, and the kite's shape, Kato believes, is exactly the same as the original of four hundred years ago. In virtually every district in which there is a continuing tradition of kite making, the kite artist faithfully reproduces the unique shape and decoration of the kite he inherits. There are generally reasons for each distinctive shape, although they are not always apparent. The peculiar shape of the Suruga kite, for example, is a result of the commonly held notion in Japan that kites requiring tails in order to fly well are not well designed.

Ask Tatsusaburo Kato to draw you one of his many designs—Kintaro, for example, the strong, young boy-god of Japanese legendary fame (Plate 45), or Yoshitsune, a popular warrior of the Genji clan (Plate 47). These are his two best sellers, kites he calls "my grand champions." When drawing these he places a sheet of paper cut in the Suruga shape on the floor and picks up a brush loaded with black ink. He looks ready, but does not immediately begin to draw; instead he pauses, holding the brush perpendicularly in the air for an instant as he considers the placement of the drawing on the irregularly shaped paper. He jabs down suddenly, the brush striking the paper hard, and with a rapid, graceful twist leaves behind an eye, nose, or mouth in strong black outline. The drawing proceeds swiftly. Next comes delicate shading in thinner washes of gray. Finally, he draws the pupils of the eyes. Each drawing of a specific face will be virtually identical to the next. Such is the skill of Kato, who at seventy-two has made hundreds of thousands of these drawings.

On subsequent visits he did several other drawings for me. One was of an *oiran*, a high-class courtesan who is normally drawn with many combs in her elaborate hair style. Kato's drawing does not include any combs. He explained the omission humorously by saying, "This is supposed to be a really naughty girl," which I took to mean that she had removed the combs to bed down with a customer. He went on to explain some details. "You probably think the head is too big, but some time ago Japanese heads were really this large. This is a very realistic drawing!"

Kato, who uses eleven colors on each of his kites, can average only three kites a day. And though the vigor of his brushstrokes and the brightness of the colors he adds cannot be reproduced in the machine-made, mass-produced kites, Kato laments the increasing numbers of low-priced imitations of his work which, despite their poor quality, give him stiff competition. A small Kato original today must sell for 350 yen, a little over a dollar.

On Boys' Day and at New Year's, Suruga kites fly over the Abe River. At the end of each festival the gay kites are returned to the shadow of a dark corner until the next kite-flying holiday comes along. For me it is as though Kato himself were being stored in some melancholy place. Of his life, Kato says: "My father loved making kites all his life and so have I, but I am always poor. Kite making is my life, but from a financial standpoint it's only a hobby." This seemingly passive acceptance is belied by the traces of bitterness in his face. When he first began making kites, his customers might say, "The eyes of Yoshitsune must look like this." This no longer happens, it seems, and he draws them as he pleases. Once, sitting with him in his shop, I discovered that his eyes strangely resemble the fierce eyes of the warrior Yoshitsune in his paintings.

Tatsusaburo Kato has no successor to continue making Suruga-dako; his three sons work as engineers for large industrial companies and none has an interest in or talent for kite making. Kato tells me that a kite maker must be skillful in working with both bamboo and paper as well as in drawing and painting. Few can master the whole range. "To become a good painter," he says, "takes several years, and mastering the paper techniques and the making of the bones requires another few years. While he's undergoing training, the apprentice gets no pay, and there are few people today who will work hard without reimbursement. Some young students recently asked me how many years it takes to be able to draw a simple circle and a straight line with a brush. When I told them two or three years they were very surprised."

He pauses for a long time, and after a moment says softly in parting, "I wish to give vigor to my kites so they might be called art." I felt he had already succeeded. Although I did not say it aloud, I thought that if I were one of Kato's sons I would continue to make the Suruga kite. But, in all honesty, I could not feel this with complete certainty.

The large Tako Hachi sign hanging above the entryway is honored for the tradition it represents, but Kato's workshop-home is small and, as a reporter friend dryly remarked, "the doors are flimsy." In order to survive, Kato must also make simple cartoon drawings for local temple festivals. His wife helps out by baking cakes, which she sells along with soft drinks at a small counter that opens from the shop onto the street. As we were leaving the shop, Kato's caged crickets began to sing, making a cheery sound that helped chase away some of the melancholy I felt inside Tako Hachi.

5

FROM SAMURAI TO KITE MAKER:
YOKOSUKA KITE MAKER MATSUTARO YANASE

T HE JOURNEY TO YOKOSUKA—a district of the town of Osuka in Shizuoka Prefecture— a short distance down the old Tokaido Road from Suruga Bay, takes one through green hills, over breathtaking mountain roads hanging far above the vast expanse of blue Pacific, over the Kikugawa (the Chrysanthemum River), and along lovely winding village roads lined with tall, soft-needled evergreen hedges, or "living walls." Here lives one of my favorite kite artists.

I have great affection for Matsutaro Yanase. I know of no other Japanese kite maker who makes a greater variety of kites: some express rich humor, others consummate beauty; some are for children, others for appreciation by adults; but all are made with superior technical skill and great finesse. All Japanese kites, Yanase's as well, are created and sold in relative anonymity. For most admirers of Yokosuka kites there is no Yanase the kite maker, only a kite that has been called *bekkako* (Plate 49), *tongari, tomoe, beka,* and several other names—or, collectively, the Yokosuka kite. All are so remarkably different that it is difficult to believe they were made by the same person.

Yokosuka kite making spans three generations in the Yanase family: Juta, Katsuta, and Matsutaro. The story of the samurai kite maker Juta that follows is told by his grandson, Matsutaro, the current Yokosuka kite maker (Plate 32). Matsutaro expresses a sense of the old feudal Japan, which, during his lifetime, has been transformed into a new modern country. For him, the dust raised in his grandfather's day by samurai feet is not too different from that raised by the Yokosuka Junior High School soccer team today. Matsutaro was fifty-eight when he wrote me the letter from which the following account is drawn.

"In the 1860s, the closing years of the Tokugawa military government, my grandfather Juta was a samurai of middle rank among the warriors serving Nishio Okinokami, the lord of Yokosuka Castle. This castle stood on a hill in the western section of town. Inside, enjoying the protection of the castle walls, was the community of Matsuo. Today the walls and the castle are gone, and all that remain are a few houses. The front of the castle was protected by a wide moat which is now a highway. At the back of the castle was the steep slope of a small mountain. As Yokosuka was a castle town, the houses on both sides of the street outside the castle walls were built at an angle to the castle entryway that permitted the samurai to stave off attack. They fought from behind each house, delaying the attackers until finally they might retreat into the castle itself. In the middle of the slope in front of my grandfather's house was an entrance gate that was barricaded at night to impede surprise attacks. Attackers never came during my grandfather's service as a samurai, but the defenders were always prepared for such a possibility.

"A samurai's training was mainly in swordsmanship, in wielding the large and the small swords. As a child, I often admired my grandfather's heavy gauntlets, his body armor, and face mask. During the Meiji era, not long before I was born, emphasis on swordsmanship in samurai training was replaced by *choren,* military drills with musical accompaniment. The soldiers also began to learn how to shoot guns and to fire cannons. A parade ground was built at the center of the western section of town, where the Yokosuka Junior High School is now located. In the eastern section of town, beyond the river, lay a flat terrace. The soldiers used to fire their cannons across the river toward a practice target on that flat land, but the balls wouldn't travel the quarter-mile distance. They always splashed in the water, to the great joy of the children who watched.

"My grandfather was still a young man prior to the Meiji Restoration, and just before the last Tokugawa shogun relinquished the powers of his military government to the emperor, Lord Nishio and his retainers moved from Yokosuka to Awa Province (part of modern Chiba Prefecture), close to Edo. Grandfather traveled in Nishio's procession on foot, his swords at his waist. The journey to Edo over the Tokaido required about one week.

"Soon after Lord Nishio's move to Awa Province, the Meiji Restoration occurred. My grandfather was then retired as a samurai and given severance pay to help establish himself as a commoner. Until his retirement, his training had been exclusively for the life of a samurai, although he had never been called upon to fight.

"For his own pleasure and that of his friends he had made kites and lanterns even while he was in Nishio's service. Upon his retirement as a samurai, he promptly decided to return to Yokosuka to establish a lantern- and kite-making business. Because kites were extremely popular throughout Japan at that time, he immediately enjoyed a thriving business, and was unable to keep up with the orders."

Matsutaro grew up listening to stories about his grandfather. Juta died in 1933, when Matsutaro was twenty-one. Matsutaro's father, Katsuta, was born in 1884 and inherited the business. A letter written by Katsuta to David Kung, who was in Japan collecting kites for an exhibition in the United States in 1960, continues the narrative of the Yanase kite makers:

"I am the second son of Juta Yanase, who was once a retainer of the twentieth lord of Yokosuka Castle. I began making kites with my father when I was thirteen years old. At that time we had many orders for kites. I learned kite making while helping my father in his shop.

"At that time we bought paper in large sheets, but nowadays we use a smaller size paper, about twenty-two by sixteen inches, made in Yamaga, Gifu Prefecture. Our bamboo, also from Gifu, is dried for more than six months after it is cut. An outline of the kite picture is drawn in *sumi* ink or with melted paraffin wax. The bright colors are made from a powdered form of water-soluble dyes that have been used since olden times.

"We make several kinds of kites. There used to be many more but today the most popular ones are the tongari, tomoe, beka, *tobi, shosuke-dako,* and the *fuwa*. A tongari (Plate 50) is long, slender, and pointed at the top. It resembles a cone-shaped hat. The kites we now make range from those made from one sheet of paper about three feet long to thirty-sheet kites nearly fifteen feet long. The designs for the tongari kite include the pine, bamboo, plum, crane, and tortoise. A tongari is flown to celebrate the birth of a baby boy.

"It was very popular during the reign of Lord Tadanao, who ruled from 1713 to 1760 as the fourteenth lord of Yokosuka Castle. My father said that Lord Tadanao, being very fond of kites, had his retainers make many different kinds. Some of the townspeople became enthusiastic about flying tongari with humming noisemakers attached. But others were annoyed by the constant noise, so that eventually noisemakers had to be prohibited. A noisemaker not only makes a loud humming sound but also enables a kite to fly well. Bamboo noisemakers produce the loudest and liveliest hum. We make them of thin bamboo shavings stretched taut by a springy bamboo bow attached to the top of the kite. This device vibrates in the wind, making an unearthly noise. We use noisemakers on tomoe and beka kites as well. The kites are bowed at the top to conform to the shape of the noisemaker.

"The tomoe design (Plate 53) has three main parts: the top part depicts the *tomoe* symbol, which is also the family crest of the first lord of Yokosuka Castle; the diamond pattern of the middle part is the "eye-tie" design, borrowed in this case from the Takaten Shrine near Yokosuka Castle; and the bottom element is a red and black war fan incorporating a circular sun and cloud patterns. The kite is made in sizes ranging from one to ten sheets of paper.

"The beka (Plates 34–35) is a small kite usually made of one sheet of paper, and is one of the most difficult Yokosuka kites to make. Despite its small size, the number of bamboo bones used varies from fifty to one hundred. Although it will fly very high and without a tail, it is very difficult to control, and a person who flies it well is considered a master kite flyer. Though many beka kites were flown in the early nineteen hundreds, very few people fly them today. Designs on this kite are quite varied; they include a Chinese lion, the peony, the tiger, a dragon, and a warrior.

"The tobi (Plate 86) is shaped rather realistically like a hawk. It has a three-dimensional head, and only one bridle string. It flies easily and well. The tobi has always been popular with children who pretend that they have a real hawk flying at the end of their string. The first Tokugawa shogun, Ieyasu, built a castle in Shizuoka Prefecture in order to pursue his great love of falconry. And we still see a great many large brown hawks in that area.

"They say there was once a man named Shosuke, who made nothing but *yakko-dako*, footman kites (Plate 84), so the lord of the castle named this kite after him. The shosuke-dako bends at the waist as it flies, and is particularly popular among small children.

"The fuwa is a kite with a warrior picture, made from three sheets of paper. In former days," Katsuta continues, "there were other designs. The type called *sukashi-dako* was a very elaborate openwork kite made by inserting slender bones in accordance with the shape of the painted design, and then cutting out any unnecessary paper in between. There were also kites called *hito-dako* which were in the shape of human beings. One of these, called *Ono no Tofu,* represented the Heian-period scholar standing with an open umbrella.

"My father, Juta, was so fond of kite flying when he was a child that people sometimes laughed at him. The kite-flying season began in May, according to the lunar calendar used in our district, and on windy days he used to run around the streets from early morning flying a kite of his own making. He was an obstinate man, and unless he was so inclined, he wouldn't make kites. I remember that we once had an order to make a big kite to be used in celebration of the birth of a child. The kite, made of one hundred sheets of paper, was so big that we had difficulty getting it out of the house. We solved the problem by rolling the kite into a cylindrical shape. In those days, it was a very common custom to celebrate the birth of the firstborn son by flying a kite. On windy days, kites practically covered the sky above our town from the middle of April to the fifth of May. I also remember that my father and I were often asked to go to neighboring districts to make paintings on kites.

"The kinds of kites I've just described are peculiar to this district, and today, outside this area, there is no one making such designs. Even people living in this area have forgotten how to make their own as they once could. My life's work has been kite making, and I wish to teach my son how to make these kites for the pleasure of future generations."

Katsuta Yanase died in 1964 at the age of eighty. His firstborn son Matsutaro is now the Yokosuka kite maker who continues to make the kites described in his father's letter.

I first visited Matsutaro in 1970 in Yokosuka. He is small, thin-boned, and slightly stooped. I can still picture him leaning over his charcoal brazier, trying to get a little extra warmth, smiling at my questions, and showing me an old family album containing photographs of his father and grandfather. A generous shock of hair, in spite of its grayness, gave him a pronounced boyish look. It was some time later that I learned he was fifty-eight. My first impression, one that still remains, is of a person without age, a kind of mythical young-old toymaker.

His workshop is simple (Plate 20), but its interior appears in complete disarray. The room is cluttered with boxes, tools, unfinished kites, stacks of paper, bundles of cut bamboo, a chest from which brushes are about to tumble out, pots with congealed globs of bright colors, and a variety of other kite materials, as well as the supplies necessary for making paper lanterns during mid-winter, when the demand for kites slackens.

If there is some sort of order, it is not apparent. It generally takes at least several years for a room to become very cluttered, and the Yokosuka shop represents almost a hundred years of accumulation. A large, dusty old tomoe kite leans against one wall. Matsutaro says his grandfather made it ninety years ago.

The workshop extends the full width of the large-sized building; its sliding doors, reaching along the entire front, face directly onto the street. The morning and afternoon sun generously brighten the room. Matsutaro works with his back to the sunlight, taking advantage of its even illumination. This way he can also avert his eyes from the distractions of the busy street outside. He sits in the middle of a raised platform, its dark brown wood worn smooth by three generations of Yanase kite makers.

His tools are surprisingly simple. No machinery is required for making paper and bamboo kites. A small clear area in the middle of the platform serves as his workbench. Aside from paints and brushes, his main tool is a short thick-bladed knife with which he splits bamboo lengthwise along the grain into strips of the required thickness. Although real skill is needed to do this quickly and accurately, the bamboo grain helps guide the knife so that nearly perfect strips result. Few kite makers make their own paper, and Yanase buys the hand-made paper of Gifu Prefecture, as did his father.

He told me that although there is no longer an organized kite festival in Yokosuka, kites are still flown in large numbers on special days. The bamboo bone work of the Yokosuka kites is among the most skillful and beautiful, and despite the fact that many people buy the kites only to look at, they are still made to be flown. The rigorous standards of craftsmanship for the flying kite remain the criteria for making and judging the finished product. How well they fly can be seen on May fifth, when boys and their fathers, anxious to show off both their flying skills and one of the distinctive Yokosuka kites, come out in large numbers.

Making a kite that can fly well is a much more demanding skill than that of satisfying aesthetic requirements. The small beka kite has both beauty and excellence of flight. Its many bamboo bones are arranged so that the larger ones are near the top of the kite, with each bone thereafter progressively smaller.

Yanase observed that a long tail would help the beka kite fly easily but would also compromise its ultimate performance. His kites must compete with those made by amateurs, and his standing as a professional is always at stake. "If I added tails," he said, "the critical eyes of the people of Yokosuka would be offended. Kite flyers would laugh and say I had made a kite that could not fly. It must fly without tails, as this is the basis upon which all the Yokosuka kite designs are evaluated."

The time required for cutting the bones precisely and for painting and then pasting on the elaborate designed paper makes the Yokosuka kites quite expensive. Prices for such kites range upward from about 14 dollars, depending on size. These kites are usually bought by adults. For the small children who often come to Yanase's shop, there is the shosuke-dako, the footman who kicks his feet like a baby and bends at the waist as he explores the sky above. The shosuke-dako sells for under a dollar.

On my last visit to Yokosuka, Matsutaro showed me a small snapshot he said was taken in 1929. The photograph was of a group of men with a coy, powdered geisha enjoying a picnic somewhere on the outskirts of Yokosuka. On one side was a young man in Western clothes, a visitor from Tokyo. This dapper figure, dressed in a vest, long-sleeved white shirt, and wide tie, and wearing a fedora, was the descendant of the lords of Yokosuka Castle. His ancestors' castle had long since disappeared, and at the time the photograph was taken, he was a major fish wholesaler in Tokyo. In the center of the photograph, in deference to his age, was Juta, the samurai turned kite maker, wearing a traditional kimono, round steel-rimmed glasses, and a stubble of beard. He towered above the rest, even as a humble kite maker, with the self-possessed samurai spirit of old Japan.

Matsutaro told me that all three of his sons enjoy painting and making kites; his eldest son will join him in making the Yokosuka kite. With his son's commitment to continue in the family profession, the slender string of the Yokosuka kite tradition will remain unbroken as it stretches from a faintly remembered past of stories and old photographs on into the unforeseeable future. In Japan, in Yokosuka, the endless sky and a frail paper and bamboo kite share an unchanging relationship as life on the earth below rushes busily by. The Yokosuka kites, once flown over the castle walls, will continue to fly over modern Japan.

6

THE INSECT KITES OF NAGOYA: SAKURAI KITE MAKER SEMMATSU IWASE

THE AREA AROUND THE CITY of Nagoya is famous for kites made in the shape of insects. The Sakurai kite (also known as Mikawa, its older name) is made about fifteen miles southeast of Nagoya, near Okazaki, a large and prosperous town on the Tokaido. Sakurai itself is a mere cluster of houses, a station on the Meitetsu Railway Line that runs through the area's flat farmlands. The sway of the train and the hypnotic clicking of its wheels made me drowsy. I was traveling around Japan on a demanding and tiring lecture tour, and I looked forward with relief to a visit with a kite maker. It was a pleasure to think of Semmatsu Iwase, the maker of the winsome bug and bee kites of Sakurai (Plates 63, 67, 68).

Iwase (Plate 33) and his wife greeted my traveling companion and me happily, but with worried looks on their faces. They were genuinely concerned that they might not have anything to offer and that my trip to see them might not be worthwhile.

Iwase is the true anonymous artist. He seemed slightly embarrassed, I thought, by my visit. Other kite makers at our first meeting had suggested with traditional—and confusing—modesty that they were not true professionals. This was also Iwase's opening remark. Actually, for me there was no doubt that he was a professional to the core. Although his kites were well known throughout Japan, not many people visited him to discuss them. "I seldom talk about this subject," he told me apologetically.

The Iwases were a handsome couple. Both had the sturdy frame and stature of hardworking farmers, the stock from which they were descended. I started off by asking him how he had become a kite maker.

"People in our district loved to fly kites," Iwase began. "At the turn of the century, there were about ten kite makers here, but kites became so popular that ten years later the number of kite makers doubled. At that time my grandfather Sentaro was a farmer. Although he had been quite prosperous and had many tenants, he lost his position due to unfortunate circumstances and had to find another way to make a living to support his six children. He was interested in kites, and with the incentive of the recent kite makers' prosperity, he chose to join their ranks. Sentaro was only fifty-two when he died. His oldest son died in the army, so my father Senjiro, his second son, continued the kite-making tradition. The rest of the family returned to farming. In my father's family, I continue to make kites. Two of my brothers are office workers, another is a farmer."

He and his wife recalled all the members of the Iwase family, past and present. They explained the meanings of the given names Sentaro, Senjiro, and Semmatsu: the suffix *taro* denotes a firstborn son; *jiro,* a second son; and *matsu,* pine. The first part of their names stems from *sennin,* the immortal beings who live isolated in the mountains, never eating, and who are said to possess magical powers.

I mentioned the well-known story of the starving but still proud samurai who picked his teeth carefully with a toothpick as if he had just enjoyed a lavish meal. Iwase laughed and agreed that his family of kite makers must resemble this samurai a little.

"Flying kites is still popular here, though," he went on. "Many of the kites we make are sold all over Japan as well. I work every day at kite making. In December my brothers join me on a part-time basis in order to help me meet the increased demand for kites at New Year's. They all enjoy kite making, but the demand for our kites is not great enough to allow all of us to work full time. We are poor, but I choose to continue my father's work."

I asked him if his son, in the first year of junior high school, would continue in the family kite-making tradition. He replied, "Yes, I think so, although he will not enjoy earning such a small income. I am afraid that only a fool can do this work," he added with a smile.

"Do you enjoy kite flying?"

"Yes, particularly the larger kites," he said. "When I have an order for a large kite I always fly it before delivering it, so that I can enjoy the results of my work."

"Does your wife enjoy helping?" I asked. She had continued to work all the while, trimming excess paper off the kites with a long-bladed knife.

She smiled and answered for herself, "I help my husband to increase our income."

When I said to her, "You are the prettiest wife of all the kite makers I have visited," she laughed and thanked me. Then Semmatsu Iwase playfully asked, "Do you really enjoy it?" and answered his own question with a yes. He reflected on the matter and added, "Maybe when we passed thirty years of age, we were better able to enjoy kite making."

There was an atmosphere of tranquillity in their home. I left them with many regrets, for Iwase was to be the last kite maker I would visit before leaving Japan.

That afternoon on the train back to Nagoya, the friend who had accompanied me observed, "You didn't feel well when we arrived at the Iwases' home, but I noticed that your face changed as soon as we began to talk about kites; you soon forgot your illness."

It was true.

7

THE NAGASAKI FIGHTING KITE:
HATA KITE MAKER SHIGEYOSHI MORIMOTO

NAGASAKI HAS PLAYED AN INTRIGUING ROLE in Japanese history as the first place that Portuguese and Dutch traders and missionaries visited in the sixteenth century in their attempts to make contact with a country that did not encourage their visits. It is a harbor city located on the northwestern coast of Kyushu, on the East China Sea. The treacherous storms that struck the Pacific coast were uninviting to foreigners who had meager navigational charts of these waters. For this reason, and because of the island's proximity to the Asian mainland, the towns of the west coast of Kyushu became natural ports of call for foreign ships. At the time, the rest of the world seemed satisfied that the goods these crowded little islands had to offer were adequately represented by the trade from Nagasaki and other Kyushu ports.

Nagasaki was formally opened as the chief port of call for Portuguese ships in 1571 and thus became the center of the *namban,* or "southern barbarian," culture. It was even for a very brief moment a free city under the administration of Jesuit missionaries. But in 1639 the Japanese government decreed that the country would be closed to all foreign visitors. During the ensuing period of isolation, lasting until 1854, only ships of the Protestant Dutch and non-Christian Chinese were permitted to call at the one remaining open port, Deshima island in Nagasaki harbor, and eventually a small foreign settlement closely regulated by Japanese officials developed on the island.

For a long historical moment, Nagasaki alone came into direct contact with the West's allurements; she slowly absorbed sciences such as shipbuilding, medicine, engineering, printing with movable type, navigation, arms making, and other technology while acting as a buffer for the remainder of Japan. The influence of this early exposure is still noticeable in Nagasaki today. Its citizens seem a little more European in their behavior than other Japanese, and though Nagasaki is not unlike modern Tokyo, it is more sedate, more settled, and more sophisticated.

The world again focused its attention on Nagasaki in 1945, when it became the site of the second atomic bombing. On the day the bomb fell, Nagasaki kite maker Shigeyoshi Morimoto had just returned to his home. John Toland, in *The Rising Sun,* a history of the Pacific war, describes that day like this: "Nagasaki, a city of 200,000, spread over precipitous hills, like San Francisco. Its bay faced the East China Sea. It was a fabled port of spectacular beauty, particularly now, for a touch of autumn had come early and many of the trees were brilliant with reddish browns and yellows. The center of town fronted the bay, which was formed by the Urakami River flowing into it from the north. With the centuries, Nagasaki had expanded from this nucleus into several valleys, including the one fashioned by the river which had become an industrial complex employing 90 percent of the city's labor force. . . .

"Shigeyoshi Morimoto was on his way home to Nagasaki, a nervous and shaken man. Only three days before, he had miracuously escaped death in Hiroshima, where he had been working for the past months making antiaircraft kites for the Army. He had been shopping for paint brushes less than 900 yards from ground zero when the bomb exploded, and the wreckage of the flimsy store protected him from the *pika* [flash]. He had fled the city, along with three assistants, in a coal car bound for Nagasaki and safety. All night long they talked compulsively about 'the bomb.' . . . By the time the freight train made its steep, dramatic descent into the Nagasaki terminal, Morimoto had an unshakable premonition that the bomb would follow him to his own home. He had to warn his wife. As he approached his shop, which was in the center of town, it was almost 11 A.M. . . .

" 'Go ahead and drop it by radar,' he [Commander Ashworth] told [pilot] Sweeney, 'if you can't do it visually.'

"The drop point, chosen for maximum devastation of the city, was on high ground near Morimoto's kite shop. An explosion here should wipe out the center of town, the port area, and reach up into the factories of the Urakami Valley. Nagasaki appeared on the radar scope at 11 A.M. . . .

"Morimoto, the kite maker, was breathlessly telling his wife that a terrible bomb had been dropped on Hiroshima and he feared Nagasaki would be next. He began to describe the *pika:* 'First there is a great blue flash—' A blinding blue flash cut off his words. He flung back a trap door in the floor and shoved his wife and infant son into their shelter. As he pulled down the heavy lid there was a terrifying tremor, like an earthquake.

"If there had been no clouds overhead, the Morimoto shop, directly under the original drop point, would have been obliterated but the bomb exploded several hundred yards northeast of the stadium and the river. . . ."

WHEN I READ ABOUT Shigeyoshi Morimoto's remarkable experiences, I decided that I would make a special trip from Korea to Japan just to meet him. My friend Kuniyoshi Munakata contacted him and arranged for the three of us to meet in the middle of November.

Nagasaki Prefecture consists almost wholly of peninsulas and six hundred or so islands. Seen from a jet, the islands look like tiny stones scattered randomly from a broken necklace. The mist rising up to us took all the color out of the scene, turning the sea a light gray hue. As we descended, the gray haze melted away, the colorless water turned deep blue, and green treetops appeared on the islands. I caught a glimpse of the city as the plane banked—from our altitude it seemed so tiny that a child's hand could hold it. At once I was caught in a struggle as I sought to comprehend the magnitude of the destruction and suffering the atomic bomb had brought this city. The paralysis that momentarily overcame me must surely strike anyone who approaches Nagasaki for the first time along the path of the B-29s. It was dusk as our plane came in for landing. The sky was filled with clouds turning pink and orange and the lights of the city, just flickering on, lay on the surface of the sea. The next morning, Munakata and I awakened to discover Nagasaki.

The Urakami River runs through Nagasaki. Halfway along its course to the East China Sea, it widens and becomes Nagasaki harbor, at which point the town spreads out to the northeast, following the smaller Nakajima River. Along the Nakajima may be found a modern business and shopping district. Two mammoth arcades are there, covered by a high, arcing canopy of colored plastic. The shopping district is crowded most of the day and late into the night, the numerous shops offering an array of goods as diverse as those of an American shopping center.

Across the harbor to the west the city is less developed, but at the edge of the harbor are the huge Mitsubishi shipbuilding yards. Other heavy industries line the shore and the harbor is usually filled with tankers, several liners, and countless small craft. An acquaintance told me that close by is a museum that depicts the holocaust caused by the atomic bomb. The crater, nearby, is covered with grass, and only a few remnants of shattered buildings remain around the perimeter. I have not gone there myself. In the rest of the city I saw no signs of the blast. I was told, by way of contrast, that in Hiroshima it is impossible to escape the monuments and damaged buildings. Nagasaki is more merciful.

Two centuries ago, farther down along the east bank, one would have seen the tiny artificial island where the Dutch traders and seamen were safely sequestered. Deshima is no longer an island, however; it was enlarged to join the main body of land, and is now the location of Nagasaki's customs house. Traces of former Dutch inhabitance are most evident in an area called the Dutch Slope, into which the Dutch finally expanded after being freed from their confining quarters at Deshima. Here, in a beautiful state of preservation, the wide cobblestone-paved lanes which were cut into a hill are bordered by sloping moss- and ivy-covered walls.

Dutch Slope is a blend of East and West, quaint and quite appealing to the eye. Japanese-style tile roofs rest above Western horizontal lap-wood siding. Double-hung sash windows replace sliding partitions, and the Western louver shutters at the windows protect them against storms. Chairs and furnishings brought from Europe used to decorate the insides of the homes. Models of the rooms as they originally appeared are exhibited in the large Dutch Slope Museum. The unusual European flavor of Dutch Slope makes it a popular Japanese tourist spot.

One of the reasons that led to the closing of Japan to foreigners was the government's concern that Christianity would sweep uncontrolled across the country, threatening native traditions, particularly the politics of the Tokugawa shogunate. The Nagasaki area was a stronghold of Christianity until the religion was proscribed in 1614. Missionaries and converts who refused to stop practicing their religion were mercilessly hunted down and given the choice of renouncing Christianity or being put to death. A small number of Christians went into hiding. Services were conducted at secret locations, generally private homes, and the faithful came to be known as "hidden Christians."

In 1597, twenty-six Christians who had been imprisoned in Kyoto were marched to Nagasaki where they were given a final chance to publicly renounce their faith. They refused and were martyred on crosses erected at the crest of Nishizaka hill, a small promontory reaching out into Nagasaki Bay. They were later canonized by the Catholic Church, and in 1864, Bernard Petijean, a French priest, erected the Oura Catholic Cathedral in their memory. This simple, white frame building is the oldest wooden Gothic structure in Japan. The wide, steep steps to its doors are often filled by the curious and the devout.

Making the rounds of the city, Munakata and I walked a short distance on down the harbor from Oura Cathedral and then back up the hillside along a meandering cobblestone lane to another landmark, the century-old estate of British merchant Thomas Glover. The grounds of Glover House were covered that day with a profusion of blossoms: lavender lilies of the Nile, yellow day lilies, azaleas, petunias, and rhododendrons. The air was heavy with their fragrance. Glover was an extremely successful businessman who had been very popular among the Japanese. He liked and admired them in return. His wife was Japanese, and Japanese visitors to his home were numerous. One frequent guest is well known in the West; the woman who has come to be known as Madame Butterfly looked out over the harbor toward the west from this garden, patiently awaiting the return of her husband. Today, Madame Butterfly stands in Glover's garden, cast in bronze. She leans slightly forward, one arm around the shoulder of her young son, the other pointing in the direction of the harbor.

BETWEEN MARCH AND MAY hundreds of Nagasaki kites fly high over the gentle slopes of Mount Inasa, across the harbor from Glover House. There is a close connection between the origin of the Nagasaki fighting kites called *hata* and the presence of foreigners. *Hata* means flag. The colors of the hata kite are red, white, and deep blue, the colors of the Dutch flag (Plates 54–56).

Sometime during the early seventeenth century, one account has it, a kite was observed flying over the walls of the Deshima settlement. Its colors and design resembled those of the Dutch flag that fluttered from the flagpole just inside the gateway. The bone structure and shape of the present-day hata kite is virtually identical to that of the fighting kite of India. Due to this marked similarity and to the fact that there is no other kite in Japan with the same design, it seems likely that the hata kite was brought from India to Japan on one of the Dutch trading ships.

The bones of the hata kite and that of its Indian precursor are simple: two crossed sticks, but cut as precisely as possible to obtain a perfect balance. Kite paper in India today, as it probably was three hundred years ago, is brittle, extremely fragile, and as thin as tissue paper. Thus, it is conceivable that when the kite-flying crewman found it necessary to replace his Indian kite paper, he modeled his design on the Dutch flag, using whatever paper was at hand. Or the Japanese, when copying the Indian kite, simply used their own stronger paper. Although the facts have long since been lost, this explanation of the origins of the hata kite seems plausible and is accepted by Nagasaki historians as a reasonable reconstruction of what actually happened.

The hata flies without a tail, as all good Japanese kites must, and with amazing agility. It is light and maneuverable in any direction. Nagasaki citizens, perhaps carried away with the kite's excellence, say that it can be flown even if there is no wind. Even more surprising, a newspaper recorded that a man named Inoue could fly a hata toward the wind although kites normally are flown against the wind. In *Kites: An Historical Survey*, Clive Hart, the dean of Western kite historians, writes that "the Nagasaki kite is probably the finest fighting kite ever designed."

A very long six-foot, two-string bridle is attached to the vertical bone. At the end of the bridle is twenty feet of line that has been coated with ground-glass paste. The main line is then tied to this rough, slightly stiff cutting line. Instead of using a reel, the kite line is fed in and out of a woven basket. The combating kite confronts its opponent from the end of 300 to 2,000 feet of string. The flyer makes his kite dip and turn in attempts to maneuver his cutting string into a position that will allow him to saw through his opponent's line. The attacked kite, meanwhile, does its best to maneuver out of danger and, if possible, counterattack.

On any of the festival days held on various Sundays in March, April, and May, great crowds of people will congregate on one of the mountains in the city. Tohakkei and Inasa are the most popular. From Tohakkei, a twenty-minute walk from the center of the city, the Ariake Sea and Mount Unzen are visible in the east; to the west lies the harbor. Inasa, overlooking the harbor directly opposite Madame Butterfly's vantage point at Glover House, commands a view of Nagasaki city, and to the west is a breathtaking view of the Goto Islands.

On the morning of the kite festival held on April twenty-ninth each year in honor of the emperor's birthday, Nagasaki harbor fills with fishing boats motoring along in loose formation, while twenty-eight-man racing shells move into position, readying for a race. Kites begin to dot the sky above Mount Tohakkei. On the mountaintop, families, kite sellers, and food and drink vendors sit under umbrellas or canvas sheets strung up to shade them from the sun's glare (Plate 30). The spectators sit on blankets or reed mats rolled out on the ground. Tiny children ride comfortably on their mothers' or older sisters' back in velvet slings that are uniquely Japanese. Soft-drink stands offer cold refreshments to accompany *o-bento* (picnic lunches), and sakè and beer are also available. The combatants' families and friends crowd around them, shouting and applauding with great enthusiasm, while boys wander through the throngs keeping a sharp lookout for falling kites. Fallen kites belong to the first person to catch them. With the cutting of a kite's string, the successful flyer shouts "Katsuro!" (cut), and as the free kite flutters downward, a race begins to claim ownership of it. The most serious of the salvagers traditionally carries a tall, thin bamboo stalk with a few limbs and leaves left at the top to help snare a falling kite before it hits the ground.

Another important gathering of kite fighters occurs during the Hata-age Festival held annually on April tenth. Hata-age kite-fighting contests follow simple rules: the contest lasts for two hours, and the kite flyer is allowed to use two kites. With the latter provision, an early defeat will not put a contestant immediately out of the competition. The contest is won by the person downing the largest number of kites during the two-hour period. The year I visited Nagasaki, the winner brought down one kite every nine minutes, for a total of thirteen kites. His prize was a silver-plated model of an old Dutch sailing ship, presented with great ceremony by a young Japanese girl in Dutch costume before the mayor and other dignitaries of the city. The prize was won, as it always is, by a serious adult kite sportsman who has probably flown the hata kite since childhood. Children compete too, but their performances are overshadowed by those of skillful adults.

In olden times the contests were probably conducted much as they are today. The techniques of cutting and the rules for claiming a fallen kite were identical, although there was no fixed season for kite fighting, nor had the flying of hata become a festival as such. Instead, kite enthusiasts challenged one another and set their own dates for fighting. Friends and relatives made picnic preparations and everyone trooped up the mountainside carrying large gourds of sakè, straw mats to sit upon, and drums to beat out rhythms for dancing and singing. Those who could afford it were served by geisha companions. Oftentimes the excitement over the fighting in the sky and the sakè in the spectators' stomachs resulted in spirited fights on the ground too. When the enthusiasm for kite flying swelled to an undesirable excess—as it often did—the authorities passed ordinances against physical combat and destruction of property by careless flyers. The government was also concerned about the disinterest in work seemingly engendered by daydreaming about kite flying. The ordinances had little effect and proved impossible to enforce in Nagasaki.

Tadao Saito, who has written a great deal about Japanese kites, states in *High Fliers: Colorful Kites from Japan*: "The strictest rule governing these hata kite fights is that the loser must bear no grudge. Ill feelings must not linger until the following day; instead, the battle must create between the combatants a link that should develop into friendship. This attitude of bloodthirsty battle contrasted by a sense of tranquillity is typical of the southern part of Japan."

Hata kites were also flown on special occasions, as when dignitaries visited Nagasaki. Former U.S. President Ulysses S. Grant visited Japan in 1879 and watched hata from a ship anchored in Oura Bay. In 1890, when a ship bearing Emperor Meiji visited Nagasaki, he sent word ashore that he would enjoy seeing hata fly. The flyers found places from which they could fly their kites within view of the emperor's ship and soon a dozen kites were in the air, including some flown by sailors from the decks of ships. Seshichi Obitana, one of the local flyers on that day, recorded his part (in *Nagasaki Hata Ko* by Kurasuke Watanabe) in what was a historical event for him and the city of Nagasaki.

"Quite a number of kites flew up from various places. A little before noon, one kite flew very high. My companions suggested that I try to cut its string. I tried it and was soon successful. Then a member of our group came running from a nearby hill, yelling that the hata I'd cut down had been flown from the emperor's ship! When we saw a sailor leap over a fence and run toward us, my friends ran away. Because I was holding the kite string I couldn't run with them, although I too was terribly afraid. The sailor came up to me out of breath and said, 'His Majesty wishes to know who cut the string of the best kite flyer on his ship.' I told him my name, my voice shaking, and he ran off as quickly as he had come. I was terribly relieved at the end of the day's happenings because I had not thought I would still be alive. Several weeks later I received a letter written by the emperor's chamberlain praising my skill at hata flying. It is my most precious possession."

WE HAD PLACED a call to Morimoto's house immediately upon our arrival in Nagasaki and had been told that we were expected in two days' time. Mrs. Morimoto mentioned over the telephone that her husband was nearly eighty and hard of hearing, so she would help in the conversation.

Zen'ichi Koga of the Nagasaki Prefectural Tourist Office, who showed Munakata and me around Nagasaki and told us a great deal about the history of the city and the hata, took us to Morimoto's home. On our way, I asked Koga what the kite maker was like. He replied without hesitation, "He is a pure Nagasaki man," and added, "Morimoto is greatly admired in Nagasaki." He tried to explain what he meant by pure Nagasaki man, but found it difficult to put into words. We had been close to Koga for several days, and it seemed to me that the term might be applied to him as well. The success of the city as a foreign port, it seems even today, is due in part to giving strangers an unshakable sense of accommodation and welcome. This Koga did graciously.

Koga said goodbye to us at the Morimoto house and returned to his office. Munakata and I were greeted at the kite maker's door by a handsome, animated young man about nineteen years old with long, curly black hair. He introduced himself as Kohei Morimoto and welcomed us to the home and workshop (Plate 94).

The workshop was a long room at the front of the house. At the rear was a raised platform, a small area corresponding to a Western living room. Along one wall was a console television and refrigerator. At a low table in the center of the room knelt a gray-haired woman who was dignified and handsome in her old age. She bowed her head all the way down to the tatami in greeting, and young Morimoto introduced her as his mother.

We were left in doubt about the relationship of Kohei Morimoto to the older man we had expected to meet, but because no explanation was immediately offered, politeness did not allow us to ask a direct question. Gradually it emerged that Kohei was most likely the recently adopted child of Shigeyoshi Morimoto. According to the traditional practices surrounding such an adoption, Kohei is held responsible for continuing the business and becomes a member of the family. He is expected to care for his adoptive parents at their retirement. Both he and his stepmother seemed reluctant to be specific about their relationship and his past. The adoption apparently canceled out his former name and life, and he was now known only as Kohei Morimoto, the hata kite maker.

Kohei was very much a professional, eager to tell us everything he could about hata. After we had exchanged calling cards, we sat down on cushions that had been placed on the tatami. Kohei explained that the long work table in front of us was used by his father, himself, and another assistant. He moved back and forth along the length of the table, reaching for one or another of the kites against the wall behind him as he enthusiastically explained the fine points of hata construction.

"The curving horizontal crossbone," he explained, "is gently heated over a candle flame to slightly decrease the tension of the bend, which would otherwise put too much stress on the kite skin. Hata are quite different from kites made in other parts of Japan. Instead of painting a design on one sheet of paper, our paper is precolored, cut, and pasted together to form the hata shape and design. We use over two hundred different designs."

He estimated that 80 percent of the designs were invented by his father, while the remaining 20 percent were either traditional hata designs or those borrowed from motifs found on clothes or other Japanese objects (Plates 95–96). "Despite the simple appearance of the hata, a variety of tasks go into its making," he continued. "The work involved varies according to the season. For example, the paper we use must be cut and dyed in summer. We also make the cutting strings at that time too.

"For the cutting element we grind up bottle glass with a mortar and pestle, then mix it with boiled rice that is not too soft. We place the glass paste carefully on the palm, cup the hand, and pass the string through the paste. Done properly, the string is given just the right degree of flexibility for flying and cutting."

He continued with a description of the seasonal breakdown of the hata kite maker's work: "In autumn the bamboo is cut to the required length and allowed to dry. The bones must be perfectly cut for balance. We trim and smooth the bamboo in the beginning of June, and continue working on it through the summer. Bones for kites to be sold in Tokyo, by the way, are cut differently from those for kites to be flown in Nagasaki. The peculiarities of the wind and relative ability of the flyers are also taken into account. We sell our kites on the banks of the Tamagawa River in Tokyo on May fifth.

"Our shop accepts orders for New Year kites until the end of autumn, and from November until January we assemble the kites. Of course we must adapt our schedule to unseasonal orders and to the weather. Wheat-flour paste is best worked in hot weather. Because of this we wait for the proper time. Our kites must fly well. Our reputation is based on their flying ability. Although many kites these days are purchased primarily for decoration, our hata are made for flying. We don't know how many, but a great number are purchased by experts or those who will become experts with experience, instruction, and good kites."

"How many hata do you make in a year?"

"Last year, 20,000," he replied, and estimated that 8,000 of these were sold in Nagasaki. The rest were sold throughout Japan and overseas. The 2,000 kites stacked behind him had just been completed for a dealer in Yokohama. Kohei seemed to be reminding himself as he said, "It requires great patience for me to sit still all day making kites."

"The kites are made to the highest degree of perfection we can attain," he continued, "so the kites must be flown with great skill in order to utilize their full potential. Here in Nagasaki there are many experts. Sometimes one of these men will help less knowledgeable flyers launch their kites, handing over the kite line once the kite is aloft. We call these men *taiko mochi,* 'scene setters,' " he said laughing. "Often the kite maker himself performs this service. Did you know that the hata is launched by throwing the kite with the wind, point first, the way you'd launch a model glider? The string is then quickly pulled back. It's really difficult. In Nagasaki, a kite flyer who has a helper hold his kite out at a distance to aid in launching it is regarded as an amateur. And kite fighting too requires great skill."

Mrs. Morimoto's job in the kite shop is to cut and tie the little paper tassels that hang from the side corners of the hata. Aside from being decorative, the primary purpose of a tassel is to allow last-minute adjustments in the kite's balance. In the field, the tassel may be trimmed to compensate for unequal absorption of moisture or other subtle variations in balance. The pretty kite made of such humble materials is in fact a precise machine.

Mrs. Morimoto had not taken part in our conversation. As Kohei talked on, it became apparent that he was now the family spokesman. When Kohei finished his explanation, I asked Mrs. Morimoto if her husband had continued a craft handed down by his father.

"Fifty years ago," she replied, "he was a carpenter by trade. But he liked hata, and was the first in the family to make kites. In the beginning, others in the family worked with him. Although they all eventually quit kite making and entered different occupations, he continued to make kites. My husband dearly loved to make kites and devoted his life to them. It pleased him when people got enjoyment out of flying kites."

As it turned out, Shigeyoshi Morimoto was ill and was not able to see us. To my great disappointment I never did see him. As we sat talking to the energetic young man who would continue the tradition of hata making, we once heard the old kite maker's footsteps moving slowly across the floor over our heads. From the front of the house there came the sound of a sliding shoji door, then footsteps returning, I guessed, to bed. From the sound of his footsteps I imagined him as an indistinct shadow. The pure Nagasaki man who wished no more of his life than to make kites of which he could be proud was, as an old Japanese verse puts it, a real man who lives many years in a few days.

8

PICNIC AT THE BATTLEGROUND: THE HAMAMATSU KITE FESTIVAL

I CAME TO JAPAN with the notion that I would learn a lot about kites—and through them a great deal about the Japanese people. As often as not, to my disappointment, my kite questions were met with bewildered surprise. Kites, I learned, were not among the everyday concerns of the average Japanese. As a consequence, I became self-conscious about my apparently peculiar enthusiasm for kites, and to offset the lack of general interest and to justify my own enthusiasm, I began to cast these fragile paper and bamboo objects as the heroes of romantic and exaggerated tales. Before I had actually seen such scenes, I created for my bemused listeners great battlegrounds in the sky where kites of indescribable beauty soared against the sun.

These fantasies, fortunately, soon came to life at Hamamatsu. There my earlier suspicion that the rest of the world was lacking a bit in its knowledge of kites was first confirmed. In Hamamatsu I found a real, living, vigorous organism called a kite—proud, beautiful, violent, and arrogant—and a city of nearly half a million people who shared my ardent enthusiasm.

To the east of Hamamatsu is Yokosuka, the home of Yanase the kite maker, and an hour farther up along the Tokaido Road lies Shizuoka city. Never long out of sight and now directly ahead, to the south, is the full sweep of the Pacific Ocean, its deep blue waters stretching as far as the eye can see, touching the sky on the horizon. Gentle waves break on the wide, black sand beach. To the west, the beach disappears into the distance. To the east, it curves slowly back on itself to create a broad spit of land. There, the sand slopes gently upward and then drops down into a large, flat arena. A very light wind blows shoreward from the ocean. Just over the rise of a shoreline dune called Nakatajima, a short walk from the ocean, preparations are underway for an afternoon kite fight.

From May third through the fifth each year, thousands of visitors throng to Hamamatsu for its three-day kite festival, one of the largest and best known in Japan. The emperor attended it in 1928, and luminaries from around the world have watched the yearly kite battles from the dune. Today, 250,000 people have gathered. The natural amphitheater was expanded by landfills, and earth-moving equipment has made parking accommodations nearby. The mile-long beach and the expansive amphitheater manage to absorb the tremendous crowd.

Square canvas stalls set out on the steeply sloping side of the dune below us ring half the field's flying area; each stall, about fifteen feet wide and fifteen feet deep, represents one of the forty-nine districts within Hamamatsu that are participating in the kite fighting. Inside the stalls, leaning against the canvas walls, are the kites, each identified by the distinctive insignia or character of the district it represents. Except for their emblems, which cover the full face of the kite, the kites are all identical in shape and construction (Plates 36, 75, 79, 88). In each stall there are about seventy-five kites in five or six sizes, ranging from the smallest, which is three feet tall, to the largest, which is fourteen feet tall. If the wind is strong, the small kites are flown; a light wind brings out the larger kites, whose greater surface areas require less wind for launching and staying aloft. The best fighting kites are thought to be in the middle-sized range. The larger kites sacrifice some maneuverability.

Hamamatsu kites are beautifully constructed. Of the bamboo frames made for large fighting kites in Japan, those of the Hamamatsu kites are the most precisely made. To provide optimum flying ability, they are made very light. The paper covering is stretched drum tight and the kite is crisscrossed with enough horizontal and vertical bones—like Japanese shoji—to make it very sturdy (Plate 91). These kites do not roll up, as do the Shirone fighting kites; the Hamamatsu bamboo frames, paper skins, and overall structure are much more refined than their rugged Shirone counterparts. While Shirone makes a cruder, and perhaps stronger and more serviceable kite, Hamamatsu over the years has drifted away from making ponderous kites toward a more artful kite requiring sophisticated, highly specialized flying paraphernalia. Style is important here. The Hamamatsu kite is considerably smaller—but still large enough to dwarf the human figures who launch it.

Amid the dust and confusion of the kite battle at Hamamatsu are many dandies, both men and kites. Team members wear distinctive, vividly colored clothing and fly colorful banners proclaiming the name of their district (Plates 28–29). Some of the elegance and pomp of courts of another era can be seen. A single Hamamatsu kite is an object of considerable beauty. The seventy-five kites in each of the forty-nine stalls ringing the flying area make an overwhelming sight for lovers of kites.

This kite festival has always leaned toward the gorgeous and lavish. As elsewhere, Hamamatsu kites were originally flown in celebration of the birth of a family's firstborn son, and families vied with each other to fly the most spectacular kite. The kite, adorned with their son's name written in one corner, expressed parental pride and hope for an auspicious future for the boy. The natural inclination of the Hamamatsu citizen was to indulge his love of kites without restraint. The feudal lords who ruled from Hamamatsu Castle, however, valued frugality and thrift. Old documents show that they constantly tried to constrain the people's kite enthusiasm in favor of the traditional virtue of austerity. In 1807 the lord of Hamamatsu Castle, for example, decreed that the kite must be no larger than four feet square. He also banned "colorful and showy designs" and ordered that eating and drinking at the celebration should be "simple and sparing."

Around 1850, near the height of the kite's popularity throughout Japan, the Hamamatsu kites were decorated with rich paintings of floating chrysanthemums, clouds, and cranes. But by the end of the century, the restrictions finally succeeded, at least partially: The lavish kite ornamentations were replaced by the relatively simply written characters of the district in which the kite originated. Emphasis on kite-fighting performance further simplified the ostentatious kite. As a consequence, the current Hamamatsu kite has a standard shape and structural framework.

Before the present-day Nakatajima flying area was developed, kites were flown in a variety of locations: from temple grounds, along the Shinkawa riverbed, or wherever people generally congregated. It was the young men of the family who purchased the kite in celebration of a relative's firstborn son and often flew it for the baby. In those days there was much drinking and revelry during the yearly Boys' Day celebration, and when the flyers' spirits were high they were easily led to regard a kite from another district as a challenge to their own. In this way, kite fighting between districts became popular. Edo-period documents record that in Hamamatsu, kites were flown over four hundred years ago, in 1558, for the birthday celebration of Prince Yoshihiro, the first son of the castle lord of Hikuma, by a retainer called Sabashi Jingoro. The evolution of organized kite fighting, from these beginnings to informal contests and then to organized kite-fighting festivals, has been gradual.

At first, one particular area became the popular gathering place for kite flyers coming from a number of districts. "Year after year," an old man told me, "the number of flyers increased and the losing kites fell, in increasing numbers, into a nearby rice paddy where they destroyed the farmer's young plants. He was at a loss as to how to protect his land until one year he hit upon the idea of fertilizing the paddy rather profusely with manure, causing the kite contestants to look for less pungent air into which to send their kites, as well as a less objectionable ground over which to pass to retrieve their fallen kites." It was this sort of incident that led to the establishment of the Nakatajima area.

The flyers from all forty-nine districts, except one, use kites made by three highly respected professional craftsmen. Two are in their seventies; the other is in his forties. Kuniyoshi Mohachi, who began learning the art of making oilpaper umbrellas at the age of ten, has spent his life working with bamboo and paper. Now he makes Hamamatsu kites. Mohachi usually employs bamboo that has been cut to the required size in November of the previous year and dried until spring, but he maintains that the lightest kites are made of cut bamboo carefully dried three years prior to its incorporation into the kite. Bones cut from the so-called female bamboo are said to be the lightest and strongest. Mohachi and the two other Hamamatsu kite makers all work full time at their profession, and independently of one another.

The smallest professionally made kites of Hamamatsu sell for 7,500 yen (about 25 dollars), and the largest for 24,000 yen (about 80 dollars). They are partially paid for by community funds, but their main source of support is contributions made by families to whom first sons have been born. Some of the families prefer not to have their kites flown believing that a bad flight or defeat in the sky is an omen of future misfortune or calamity for their son. These families hang the kite from the ceiling of their child's room. Less timid parents, I suppose, follow the progress of the fighting kite bearing their son's name with some nervousness.

IN THE ONE DISTRICT that makes its own kites, two middle-aged brothers who possess special skills supervise many helpers in the construction. The brothers, Seiichi and Heizo Ito, are owners of a small noodle and *tofu* (bean curd) factory in their district. It is a factory distinguished for its secret family recipes and the old-fashioned worn wooden vats and implements used in the kitchen. But being genuine kite addicts, they are always ready on very short notice to abandon their work and talk about kites, as they did on the day of my visit.

We walked first through the ground-floor workshop where the noodles were made, then up a narrow flight of stairs to the living quarters. In a room surrounded by high-fidelity equipment—of special interest to a teen-age son well versed in classical music—we sat and talked about kites. Smaller children frequently came and went, so that it was difficult to know who was whose child. Once one of the girls brought in her classmates to listen to me speak English. Both Munakata and I tried to cajole them into speaking English. We couldn't break through their shyness, however, though they were serious enough about hearing "real" English—which they were studying in school—that they were not about to retreat.

"Has your district's kite won often at the yearly festival?" Munakata asked one of the brothers.

"The numbers of kite-flying teams have increased to such an extent that the kite association has decided against naming a winning district. Prizes for first, second, and third place were the cause of many disputes and ill-will."

"Are there ever any women on the flying teams?" I asked.

The elder brother, Seiichi, answered, "No, never. It requires a great deal of stamina and strength to fly these kites. Some members, of course, are stronger than others, and they are placed where the greatest strength is required; young boys who may not be very strong are placed between the older members. This allows the younger ones to learn kite-flying techniques. None of the participants train or practice prior to the festival. Younger members learn by working with the team during the festival."

"How is a kite's line broken during a kite fight?" I asked. As the brother explained the peculiarities of the Hamamatsu lines and cutting techniques, one of the girls was sent off for a ball of kite string, which she presented to me with a little dip of her head.

"The main flying line of the kite, as well as the bridle lines, are made of twisted flax grown in Shinshu [Nagano Prefecture]. The flying line is attached to thirty-six lighter bridle lines that are spread evenly across the face of the kite. Among these thirty-six lines are three slightly lighter bridles, one at each of the upper two corners of the kite, and one fixed just below the center. A kite attacks by bringing its flying line across the opponent's two corner bridle lines. Friction caused by the flying line moving across these weaker lines will break them relatively easily. When broken, the sudden unequal stress on the other lines will cause them all to snap, and the kite is separated from its flying line. The attack may be made from either above or below, but the higher kite has a slight advantage. In the end, though, the superior dexterity of either flyer will determine the ultimate victor."

"The flying line has the same thickness regardless of the size of the kite being flown," Heizo continued where his brother had stopped. "If our flying line were heavier, it would reduce the maneuverability of the smaller kites. This also means that we cannot fly larger kites on windy days. We prefer to fight with medium-sized kites, which are the most maneuverable and ideally suited to the flying line. The different kite sizes allow us to adapt immediately to changes in wind conditions."

"The single flying line accommodating a variety of kite sizes does not compromise our flying ability significantly enough to warrant the expense of elaborate equipment and additional diameters of flying line," Seiichi observed.

"How are the techniques of kite construction passed along?" I asked.

"Generally by apprenticeship," the older brother said.

His brother added, "There are also some written works on the subject. Several years ago, for example, Mr. Suzuki was successful in making a kite requiring only twenty-seven bridle strings. He has become famous since then, having written a book, *Itome-tsuke Hiden* [How to Fix Bridle Strings: The Secrets]. The kite association keeps several such documents, although practical experience over a long period of time through apprenticeship and one's own efforts produce the best results in kite flying. There are many secrets in regard to the construction of the Hamamatsu kite and its flying techniques. Some of these secrets are not well kept, since we also would like our competitors' kites to perform well."

Kite making and kite fighting will not disappear from Hamamatsu in the foreseeable future. There are too many people whose enthusiasm for kite flying at festival time knows no bounds. Mohachi, the seventy-four-year-old bamboo craftsman-kite maker says, "I am still fascinated by the fresh greenness of bamboo and feel challenged to make a gallant kite. Even now I look forward, like a small child, to the kite festival." It would not be an exaggeration to say that hundreds of thousands of people look forward to those three days in May when so many kites may be seen together in the sky.

INNUMERABLE SMALL DOTS filled the blue sky over Nakatajima beach. One kite moved slowly over and across those that appeared to be fixed in the sky. Occasionally a kite broke away from the invisible line connecting it to the earth. Free of the restraining line, it soared toward the sun for a short eternity of freedom before gravity brought it downward, drifting back and forth, until it finally disappeared into the top of a grove of pine trees.

We were driving toward the beach in a slow-moving line of traffic; the road was packed with cars going to the festival. On this day we were guests of the Omura family. Japanese from all walks of life attend the festival. Shinzo Omura, for example, is the president of several businesses in Hamamatsu, and he and his family live in a spacious modern house. Although there are very few private planes in Japan, he flies a small plane in his leisure time. Their teen-age daughter acts much as a typical American teen-ager. The family is a thoroughly modern one that has grown up with the kite festival—and still enjoys it.

The kites' flying lines were barely discernible as we drew closer to the arena. They disappeared into a cloud of dust that swirled about close to the ground. The sound that reached our ears was an eerie caterwaul punctuated by the blasts of a cornet and by shouting and cheering voices. As we walked closer still, the overall effect was the likes of which I have never experienced.

Our group spread a blanket on the beach and with a restraint I was barely able to manage, I tried to enjoy a leisurely lunch. But the sounds of merriment in the flying area just out of sight over the sand embankment were pulling me like a magnet. Though the Omuras guaranteed that the festival would be there until late in the afternoon, I soon drifted away from the beach picnickers and walked toward the kite fighting.

In the center of the arena, raising the cloud of dust we had seen from the distance, are the kite-fighting teams. Each team has up to fifty members dressed in colorful coats, sashes, and headbands bearing the same design and colors as their district's kite. The members hold aloft similarly designed banners on tall bamboo poles, the cloth flapping in the swirling dust. With them in the arena is a milling crowd of festival visitors: photographers, newsmen, neighborhood fans, and families whose firstborn sons' kites battle overhead. Kite lovers, young and old, add to the commotion. Although the majority of them watch from the safety of Nakatajima sand dune, viewers are not restricted from the center of frenzied activity. The more adventurous enter the battle area and, in the confusion and dust, become almost indistinguishable from the teams of flyers.

The kite teams carry their kites to the far side of the field, holding them high above their heads and parallel to the ground, safe from possible damage by the crowd. They set the kite upright against poles to straighten and untangle the bridle strings. When the many bridle lines are in position, a drumlike reel (Plate 27) fixed to a two-wheeled cart plays out a long length of flying line. As long as a kite flies well, the men who operate the rather complicated-looking reel have an easy job. The reel's main function is to store the unused line and keep it from becoming impossibly tangled. Each team's bright banners fly from its reel station. And it is here that older team members and small children cluster, safe from the reckless flyers and the excited crowd.

At the rear of the field, a kite is ready. A long bamboo pole, twice the height of the kite, extends vertically through its middle axis. Three rope tails—their lengths will vary from sixty-five to one hundred feet, depending upon wind conditions—are tied to the end of this pole. Generally speaking, the Japanese feel that very large kites and tiny kites often require tails, whereas medium-sized kites should fly well without tails. About twenty flyers stand at intervals along the flying line. These are the linemen. One or two flyers raise the kite up into the air, hoisting it high over their heads by grasping and then shoving the long center pole upward. At the command of the team leader, they release the kite and the linemen dash across the field, running at full speed while shouting encouraging words to each other at the tops of their voices. The long flying line lifts diagonally off the ground, its hemp tails flailing the air over the heads of the crowd with a frightening whistle as the kite moves into the sky (Plate 90).

After their initial sprint, some of the linemen drop the line and run toward the kite. They grab the line again with both arms and, bending their bodies, vigorously pump the line up and down. These sudden jerks help raise the kite farther up into the sky where air currents will hold it aloft. At the leader's command they run forward again and again, tumbling over each other in their excitement and plunging through the crowd, which has been unable to move out of their path quickly enough, until the kite flies steadily above.

Some kites come crashing down unexpectedly into the churning mob. A frightening roar of paper parting the wind sends people scurrying out of danger. The kite hits the ground with the sounds of cracking bamboo and ripping paper. Amazingly, no one is seriously injured during this festival.

The crisscrossed lines lying on the ground are the most dangerous of the field's many hazards, for they can suddenly snap to life and catch someone's foot. My ten-year-old daughter was burned on the neck by one of these suddenly rising lines. The small scar she bears will remind her for a while to come of the dangers of the Hamamatsu kite battleground. The burn, however, has not dampened her enthusiasm for kite flying.

The successful flying of any kite depends chiefly on interpreting the *feel* of the wind hitting the kite through the kite-flying line, although fifteen to thirty men holding the line with all their strength are too coarse an instrument to receive this delicate message. Simply put, the message is: when the wind blows, let out your string; when the wind slackens, bring it in. One man at a position called the *itosaki,* literally string edge or the position closest to the kite, makes these decisions (Plate 92). When he shouts "Pull," the linemen grab the line and, with all their strength, run pulling the kite against the wind their running creates. His shout of "Stop" brings them falling to the ground gasping for breath. And at a cry of "Let out," those manning the reel release the brake, allowing the line to play out. All commands are repeated over a brass cornet that penetrates the terrific din. To avoid confusion, each team uses it own distinctive signals.

While the kite soars freely, the man called the point man anchors it to the earth. This man is the strongest in his district; he, in turn, is held tightly about the waist by one or two more strong men, all of them sitting on the ground (Plate 89). The kite line passes through a metal pulley that the point man grips tightly with both hands. At the command to pull in, his helpers grab him about the waist and he digs his heels into the ground and leans far back against the sudden pressure of the wind hitting the kite. The line, pulled in by the other twenty or so members of the team near him, passes through his pulley and drops to the ground as it comes down out of the sky.

The extra flying line left lying on the ground serves as a buffer between the storage reel and the linemen. It can be quickly let out again if the wind catches the kite and it can be used to place the kite in an advantageous fighting position or to beat a hasty retreat from attack. The line is pulled in to the rhythmic chant of "Yoi-sho, yoi-sho, yoi-sho!"

At the rear of the flying area, stretched twenty feet above the ground between sturdy poles, is a taut horizontal cable that breaks the fall of kites approaching the ground. The angle of the kite's line in relation to the earth diminishes as the kite descends, but when the line suddenly crosses the cable, the kite immediately rises again. A kite line racing across this taut wire produces an alarming shriek similar to the sound of a thousand out-of-tune violins. Some kites are not affected by the wire's lifting effect and, continuing their fall, land in a grove of pine trees.

At the far end of the field, where the kites are first lifted up into the air and where the well-being of the flyers as well as that of the viewers seems most perilous, the exhilaration felt by the Hamamatsu citizens is at a fever pitch. Everyone is dust-coated from top to bottom and seems to be shouting. Kites lift quickly off the ground. A team of twenty linemen runs madly pell-mell through the crowds. A shrill blast from a cornet pierces the air. Smoke rises from shrieking flax lines that race over the high steel cable, and lines crisscrossing the ground jump unexpectedly to life.

In the middle of the swirling pandemonium, one tako-kichi walks aimlessly, his face a broad grin, his eyes beneath dusty lashes glazed over in near-complete ecstasy at being able to participate in this kite fantasy come to life. Above him a single defeated kite, cut free of its line, floats quietly away toward the horizon and the setting sun.

9

THE TASTE OF KITES:
CONSUMMATE COLLECTOR SHINGO MODEGI

Buddhism teaches that suffering is inherent in life; only through mental, moral, and physical self-purification can one escape this suffering while on earth. To an outside observer, the enlightenment that results from this ordeal is often evidenced by the open, smiling faces of Buddhist priests, men who also seem to have the ability to laugh easily.

When Shingo Modegi, one of the world's greatest kite enthusiasts (Plate 93), is talking about kites, he literally never stops smiling, and his eyes reveal almost constant astonishment. Wide-eyed wonder, consummate enjoyment, and love are strong feelings to express for any length of time. I have asked many Buddhist priests, including several high-ranking Zen masters, if they have any knowledge of or enthusiasm for kites. Their answer, invariably no, is puzzling: puzzling because, to me at least, it appears that Modegi has found a method of achieving enlightenment as yet untried in traditional Buddhism. Whether this kite enlightenment is genuine or exists only in my imagination is unimportant to me. Modegi is respected by Japanese kite enthusiasts as one of the few experts on Japanese kites. He is particularly admired for introducing this knowledge, with love and contagious enthusiasm, to kite enthusiasts throughout the world.

To kite enlightenment we might add "food enlightenment," for Modegi is the owner and chef of one of Tokyo's best European-style restaurants, the Taimeiken Restaurant in the Edobashi district, a short walk from Tokyo Station. Every day, from early morning until late at night, Modegi can be found supervising the kitchen staff of his large and very successful restaurant. One first notices his childlike smile and then his peculiar posture: a body gently curved in a soft S, like the branches of a willow; at sixty his body reflects the years of constant bending in the kitchen. The smile is not one of childlike innocence, but an old man's innocence retained despite a long life of cooking, managing a successful business, and flying kites.

Modegi's father, a pharmacist, also liked kites. The family lived in urban Tokyo so there were few opportunities for Modegi to fly kites. As a result, his enthusiasm increased daily as New Year's Day approached. Modegi's father would drink a lot of sakè while he and the children waited each year for the kite maker to finish his work. The wait at the shop made them drowsy, and to keep them awake the kite maker would always say, "If you fall asleep before hearing the temple bells toll one hundred and eight times [to rid the hearer of various human desires], you will lose all your hair!" To give his story further weight, he added that his own bald head was the result of failing to stay awake.

Kite flying was a serious activity for children then, an art to be done with the greatest possible skill. In December, children rehearsed with small, cheap, bridleless kites that they bought with their own money. On New Year's Day, Shingo's father always bought his boys a big kite, about six feet square, which they all took to a nearby field to fly. New Year's kite flying lasted all day long and, under the guidance of his father and brothers, the small boy learned to fly well. He continued flying them during his junior high school years, but then the family's fortunes went into a decline and he had to quit school and go to work.

"I was poor and thin then, and I often thought about eating. I decided to run a Western-style restaurant because I wanted to become fat," he explained, adding, "There were fifteen in our family."

Modegi found work in a Western-style restaurant, but as he tells it, "My master didn't permit me to eat too much at first. To occupy my mind I occasionally flew kites from the restaurant balcony. One day the owner shouted up at me to return to work immediately. I was too afraid to pull the kite in, so I tied the string to the railing and left it flying. That night I returned and found the string in the dark. Although I couldn't see it in the darkness, the kite was still flying." He made a gesture of pulling in the kite string hand over hand, jumping up from his chair to emphasize the idea of something being far overhead in the sky.

"It was a very strange feeling," he continued, "not being able to see the kite in the pitch blackness, but being able to feel it pulling against the wind. Suddenly it hit against my face and frightened me badly. I hurried away home feeling relieved that my kite was safely under my arm."

His story jumped ahead to the years of the World War II. "Before the war we could always see kites flying at New Year's, but not during the war, nor for a long time after it. Nevertheless, I continued to fly the happy yakko-dako, the Edo, and the Shirone rokkaku kites, hoping their sight would provide some relief from the war, and from the sadness that hung over Tokyo during the postwar period."

When you visit the Taimeiken Restaurant with a kite-enthusiast friend, Modegi will invariably come to your table to ask questions about kites. He will often bring his newest acquisition, say, a new plastic kite he has received from a friend in another country. And this he'll leave with you while he returns to his work. Modegi works till late at night and is one of the last to leave. As he goes, he often carries a half-dozen different kites taken from his collection of hundreds from around the world. These he will try to fly before going to bed, if it is a moonlit night, or early the next morning before returning to work.

In 1965 he thought it might be interesting to fly Japanese kites in Paris. Upon climbing the Arc de Triomphe with an armful of kites, he made preparations for flying them. He was immediately chased away by a gendarme. Undaunted, he walked on down to a plaza near the Eiffel Tower and there spent the whole day flying yakko-dako and several Shirone rok-kaku kites with the help of young and old Parisians who had never seen Japanese kites before, much less kite flying next to the Eiffel Tower. Children watching said they thought the Japanese kites were higher than the Eiffel Tower; other spectators told him he was probably the first person to fly such kites in Paris.

Modegi related these events while leafing through a gold-edged, very worn and small leather-covered volume in which I could see he had written notes and sketched kites, along with well-drawn food arrangements and pastry designs. "There were many good recipes for pastry in France," he added with a laugh.

From there he went to Kensington Gardens in London, where he found many English-men flying kites. Modegi speaks little English, but he has a strong handshake, uncommon in the land of the bow, and he was warmly welcomed when he asked to join the English kite flyers.

At the New York World's Fair he flew kites from the roof of the Japanese pavilion. "But I was not noticed by many Americans, except for one fact. I'm a fan of Micky Mantle and so I wore a Yankee baseball cap. Several people shouted 'No Yankees!' so I thought it might be a good idea to remove it, but an American told me it wasn't necessary," he recalled.

In 1969 he flew his kites in Beirut and then, on his way back to Paris, traveled along the coast of Normandy, where he flew kites at numerous port cities along his route. Again he visited Kensington Gardens ("Perhaps the first person to fly Japanese kites twice there," he says) and then returned home by way of Taiwan, "to fly kites in Chinese skies." He fondly recalls a day in Paris when "A small boy told me, 'Please come again on a windy day!' I would like to return."

Modegi helped found the Japan Kite Association in 1969 with Tadao Saito and Yusaku Tawara, authors of several books on Japanese kites. There are now over 1,000 members, who meet twice a year at the Taimeiken Restaurant. They also fly their kites on the banks of Tokyo's Tamagawa River on Boys' Day each year. "People may see at one time kites from every district here, as well as many tako-kichi," Modegi says. "Our association has no officers, no dues, and no rules, as we are all gentlemen. The members are men, mostly older men, from many professions: poets, painters, university scientists. It is a pleasure to share the joy we receive from kites."

Shingo Modegi in the prime of life—smiling face, a bit of a Buddha with a strong hand-shake—is a self-appointed ambassador. Tied to the worn traveling bag he carries is a long string that reaches into the sky, and at the end of it is a beautiful Japanese kite.

PORTFOLIO OF KITES

Notes on this portfolio section follow on page 113.

37

38

39

40

41

42

43

44

45

大蛇丸

46

47

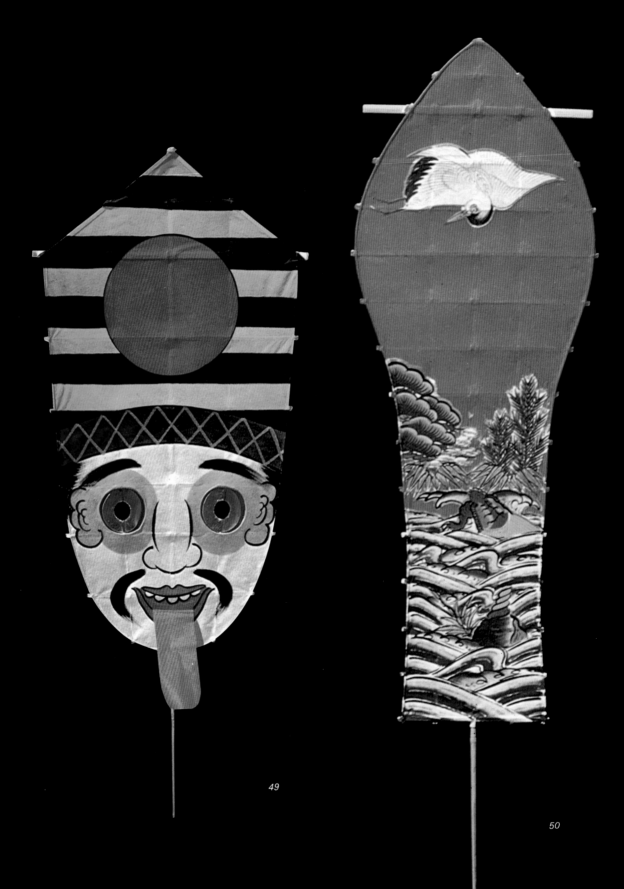

49

50

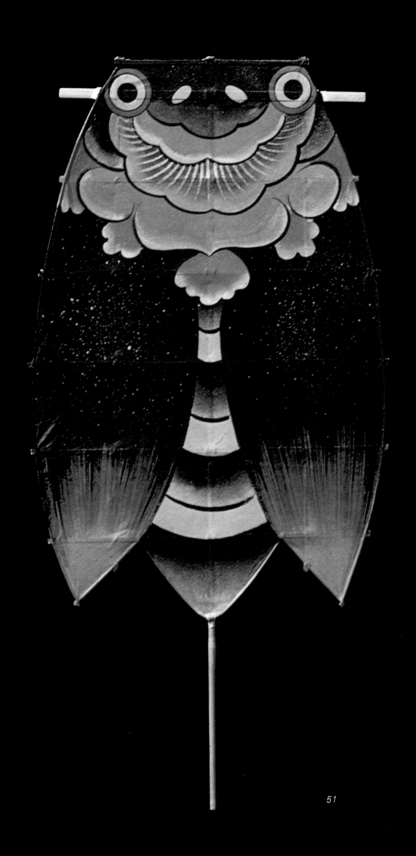

51

52

53

54

55

56

57

58

59

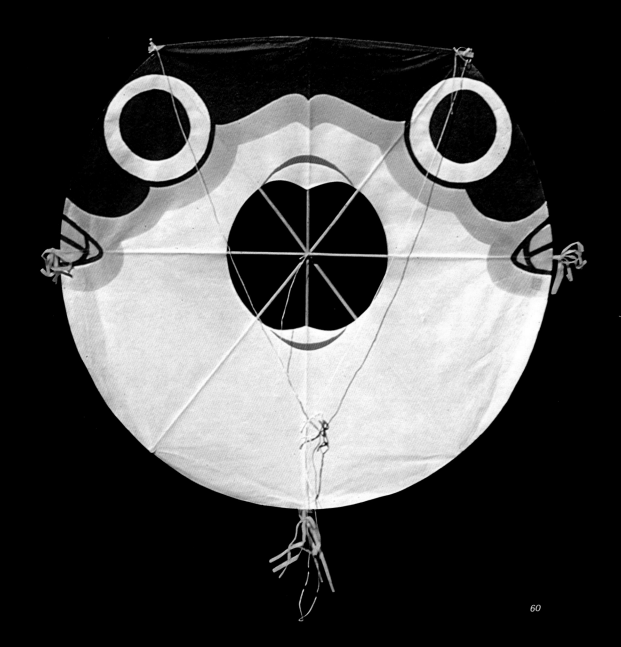

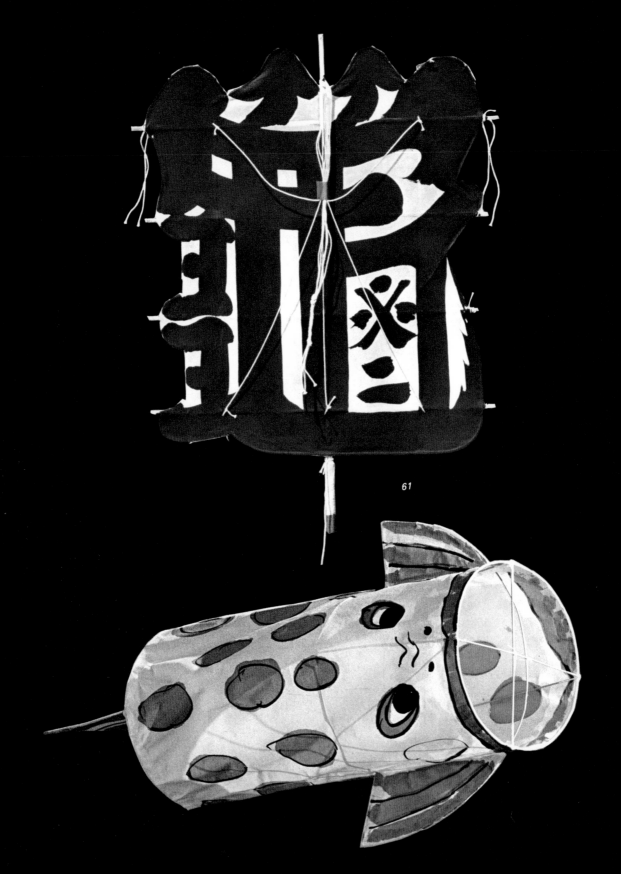

61

62

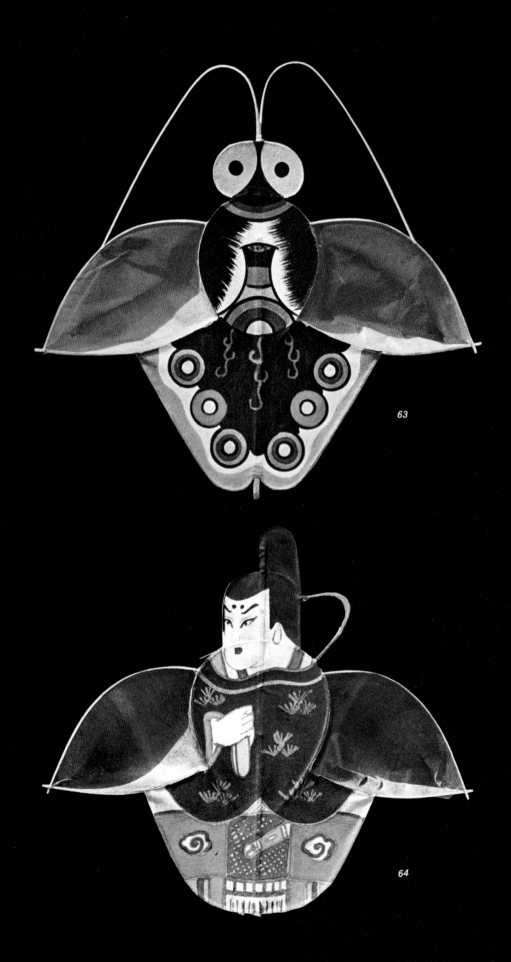

63

64

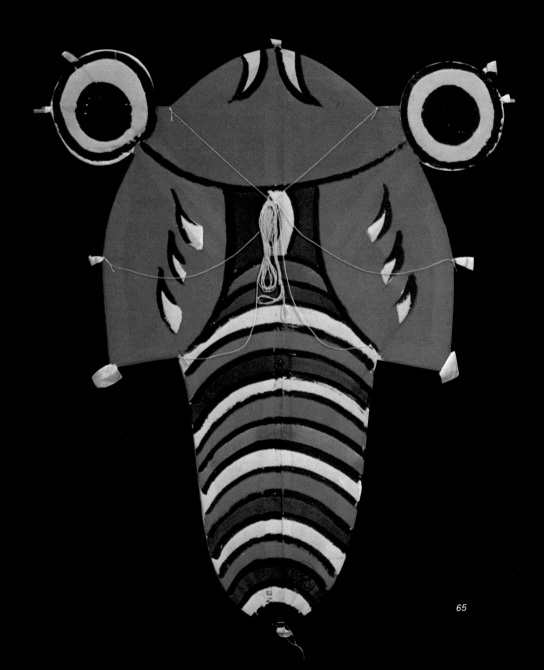

65

66

67

68

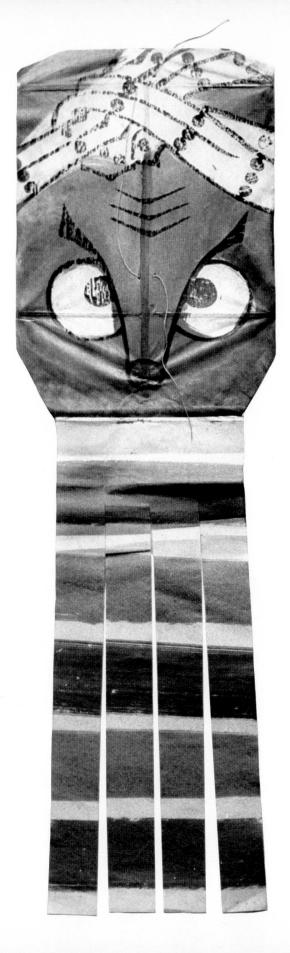

70

71

72

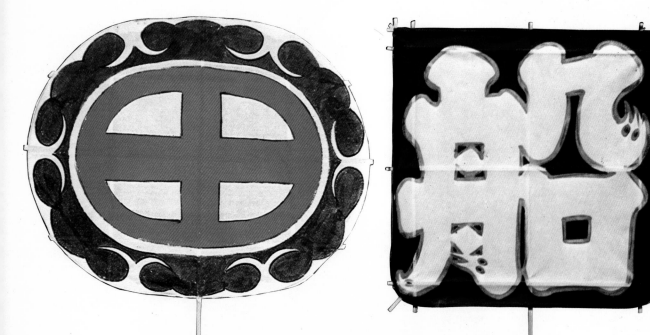

74

75

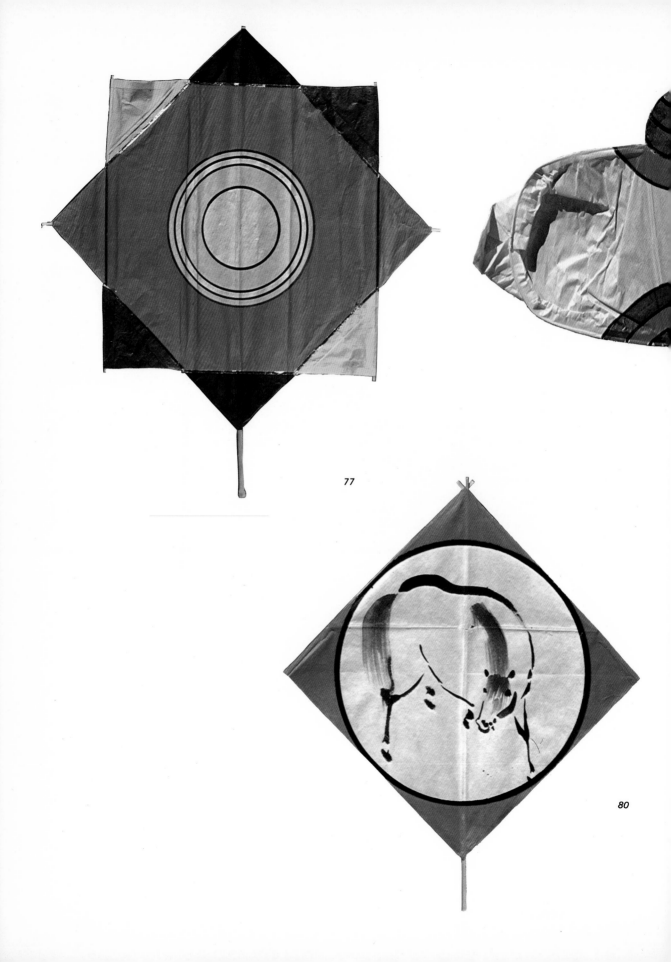

77

80

78

79

81

82

83

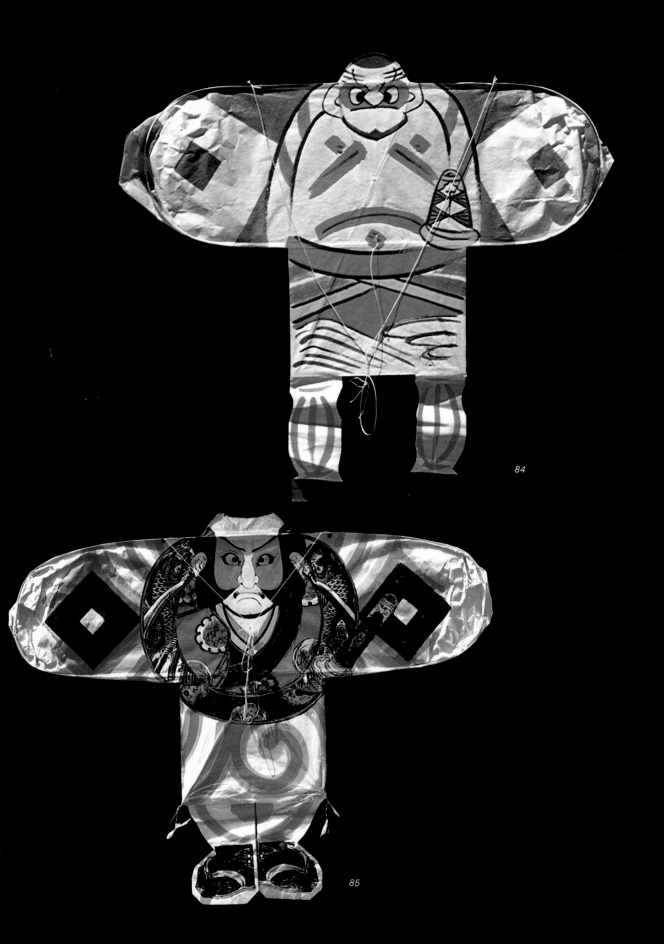

84

85

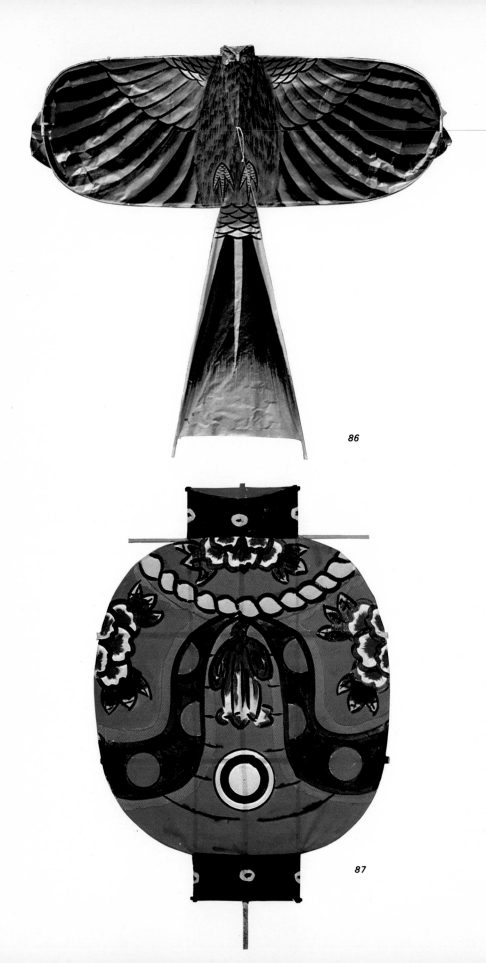

86

87

NOTES ON THE
PORTFOLIO OF KITES

37. Sanjo kite portraying Minamoto no Tametomo. Tametomo was a twelfth-century warrior said to be possessed of Herculean strength. He was banished to an island off Izu by an emperor supporting the rival Genji clan. One of the many legends surrounding his life while in exile relates to an attempt to return his son to the mainland via a giant kite. See also Plate 114. By Toranosuke Watanabe, Shirone, Niigata Prefecture.

38. A hexagonal kite depicting a Kabuki actor in the role of a feudal-age warrior. By Toranosuke Watanabe, Shirone, Niigata Prefecture.

39. A hexagonal Sanjo kite portraying a Kabuki actor as Oishi Yoshio, leader of the celebrated Forty-seven Ronin. By Toranosuke Watanabe, Shirone, Niigata Prefecture.

40. An outstanding Edo kite with wave motif. By Teizo Hashimoto, Tokyo.

41. An Edo kite portraying a warrior. By Teizo Hashimoto, Tokyo.

42. An Edo kite with a complex design of two mounted warriors in full armor. Such kite paintings are often called *nishiki-e,* brocade picture, a reference to a painting style derived from ukiyo-e woodblock prints. By Teizo Hashimoto, Tokyo.

43. Daruma kite, depicting the Indian Zen sage Bodhidharma. The fierce eyes for which the Daruma is famous are effectively portrayed. By Teizo Hashimoto, Tokyo.

44. A distinctively shaped Suruga kite, with a fierce warrior design. The first Suruga kite was flown in the early 1500s as a symbol of victory in battle. By Tatsusaburo Kato, Shizuoka.

45. A Suruga kite showing the golden boy Kintaro and a carp. Such kites are often flown on Boys' Day. The upstream-going-carp is a symbol of strength and success, while Kintaro is known as a strong and healthy boy. By Tatsusaburo Kato, Shizuoka.

46. A Kabuki actor wearing traditional makeup for the role of a warrior adorns this Suruga kite. The shape of this kite has remained unchanged for over four centuries. By Tatsusaburo Kato, Shizuoka.

47. A Suruga Yoshitsune kite. Minamoto no Yoshitsune, brother of Yoritomo, who established a military government in Kamakura, is legendary for his feats of bravery and prowess. This kite, along with the Kintaro, are kite maker Kato's bestselling kites. By Tatsusaburo Kato, Shizuoka.

48. Kite with rabbit and surging waves motif. This design is probably taken from the old belief that the female rabbit conceives by running on the waves on the eighteenth day of the eighth moon if the sky is clear. By Teizo Hashimoto, Tokyo.

49. This *bekkako* kite depicts the *saru mawashi,* or monkey showman, who appears in Yokosuka at New Year's with a performing monkey. He is said to bring humorous entertainment as well as good luck for the coming year to the families he visits. The stuck-out tongue is identical to the derisive American gesture. By Matsutaro Yanase, Yokosuka, Shizuoka Prefecture.

50. A *tongari,* a pointed celebration kite. This kite is laden with symbols for a propitious life for a firstborn son: crane and long-tailed tortoise for longevity, pine and bamboo for longevity and resilience. This kite ranges from three to fifteen feet long. By Matsutaro Yanase, Yokosuka, Shizuoka Prefecture.

51. A *semi,* or cicada, kite. The song of the cicada which so marks hot summer days is a favorite of all Japanese. By Matsutaro Yanase, Yokosuka, Shizuoka Prefecture.

52. Mori *buka* kite made by Shin'ichi Muramoto who also makes folk toys. This upstream-going-carp design is one of the most dramatic of kite paintings and appears only on large, specially ordered kites. The "buka" of its name refers to the sound the kite makes when rising into the air. From Mori, Shizuoka Prefecture.

53. The *tomoe* kite has a three-part design. At the top is the *tomoe* symbol composed of three twirling commas, at the center are two "eye-tie" textile designs, and at the bottom is a folding fan incorporating a circular sun and cloud patterns. By Matsutaro Yanase, Yokosuka, Shizuoka Prefecture.

54. A Nagasaki *hata,* a fighting kite noted for its deceptively simple design and superb maneuverability. By Shigeyoshi Morimoto, Nagasaki.

55. A tricolor Nagasaki *hata* with a circular sun and wave motif. By Shigeyoshi Morimoto, Nagasaki.

56. A Nagasaki *hata* with a tricolor design of a shore bird flying over highly stylized waves. By Shigeyoshi Morimoto, Nagasaki.

57. A Sanjo kite portraying Uesugi Kenshin, the sixteenth-century warrior who is also known as a distinguished Buddhist priest. By Toranosuke Watanabe, Shirone, Niigata Prefecture.

58–59. A diamond-shaped kite, the Tosa-bishi, with a design of a helmeted warrior and the ogre he battles. The crossbone of this kite is easily removed and the kite can be folded to the shape on the right for easy carrying. From Kochi Prefecture.

60. A *fugu* (blowfish) kite from Shimonoseki, Yamaguchi Prefecture. The blowfish, which can often be poisonous, is considered a delicacy in Japan.

61. Izumo *iwai* kite. *Iwai* means "celebration," and the ideograph on this kite stands for *kame,* or "tortoise," an animal that symbolizes longevity. From Taisha, Shimane Prefecture.

62. A Fukuoka *donko* kite. This unusual three-dimensional tubular kite is made in the shape of a *donko,* a fish that rarely moves, and lives in small streams and rice paddies. The kite maker, Masato Fujita, of Fukuoka Prefecture, enjoys experimenting with a variety of shapes instead of following local traditions.

63. A *cho,* or butterfly, kite. By Semmatsu Iwase, Sakurai, Aichi Prefecture.

64. Sakurai Tenjin kite. Tenjin is the posthumous title given to the ninth-century courtier Sugawara no Michizane, who is pictured here in court dress. From Sakurai, Aichi Prefecture.

65. The cicada design was a favorite of Magojiro Takeuchi, a kite maker of Kitakyushu, who gave his name to this Magojiro *semi.* Takeuchi drew in a distinctive, wildly expressive style in a very appealing childlike manner. The *semi* illustrated here follows the original Magojiro design but as it was executed by his successor, the brushwork has tightened up into the more conventional mode of kite drawing.

66. Takuma *semi,* a cicada kite from Takuma, Shikoku. By Natsue Isozaki.

67. The *tobi,* or hawk, kite. By Semmatsu Iwase, Sakurai, Aichi Prefecture.

68. Fukusuke, a large-headed dwarf who brings good luck. By Semmatsu Iwase, Sakurai, Aichi Prefecture.

69. A block-printed octopus kite made in 1934. This is a double *tako* as both the kite and octopus are pronounced "tako" in Japanese. The octopus wears a *hachi maki* towel tied around its forehead in a manner common to artisans, laborers, and festival participants. From Sanjo, Niigata Prefecture.

70–71. Two Tsugaru kites. The Tsugaru is the only Japanese kite with bones made of material other than bamboo. Its bones are of *hiba,* a kind of heavy cypress. Thus a strong wind is necessary to fly this kite. Tsugaru kites are highly prized for the quality of their paintings, usually of famous warriors. Tsuzan Yoshitani, who lives in Hirosaki, Aomori Prefecture, is one of the finest Tsugaru kite artists.

72. Nambu-Hachinohe Kintaro. There are three similar kites made in the northeast prefecture of Aomori: the Nambu, Aomori, and Tsugaru. The Nambu Kintaro bears one of the most winsome designs of the golden boy who appears as a favorite figure in kites all over Japan. Aomori kites carry paintings of popular Kabuki actors. Both utilize a framework of standard bamboo and are good flyers.

73. A *sumotori* kite in the shape of the traditional Japanese wrestler. Around his waist he wears the thick twisted rope *(yokozuna)* that signifies his championship rank. From Kagawa Prefecture.

74. A small *wanwan* kite made by Mampei Tadokoro of Naruto, Tokushima Prefecture.

75. A Hamamatsu fighting kite with the ideograph *fune* which means "boat." From Hamamatsu, Shizuoka Prefecture.

76. A *karuta* kite. The design has been borrowed in its entirety from one of the playing cards of the flower card game *hanafuda,* in which each month is represented by a plant. This is the August card, with a highly stylized design of pampas grass and a full moon. From Bungo Takada, Oita Prefecture.

77. A *hakkaku,* or octagonal, kite with bull's-eye pattern. From Takamatsu, Kagawa Prefecture.

78. This kite, a *koma,* is based on a Japanese top, from which it also takes its name. From Bungo Takada, Oita Prefecture.

79. A Hamamatsu kite. Simply but strikingly designed, these fighting kites were originally used to celebrate the birth of a first son. From Hamamatsu, Shizuoka Prefecture.

80. A Tosa *harukoma,* by the late Hanzo Yoshikawa of Tosa, Kochi Prefecture. Well known for his graceful, economically drawn horse (*harukoma* means "spring colt"), Yoshikawa had many admirers and students. A successor has taken his name as the Tosa kite maker.

81. A Tosa *jomon,* or family crest, kite. The design is of a stylized plum blossom in a circular enclosure. From Tosa, Kochi Prefecture.

82. A *sode,* or kimono, kite. The name literally means "sleeves," but refers, in this case, to the entire garment. The design is of a fierce-looking dragon. From Honno, Chiba Prefecture. Courtesy of So Kobayashi.

83. A kimono kite from Honno, Chiba Prefecture, with a design of Kintaro and the strong carp. Courtesy of So Kobayashi.

84. A *shosuke yakko* kite. This kite is said to have been named after Shosuke, a kite maker who made only *yakko* (footman) kites. It bends at the waist as it flies, and is particularly popular among children. By Matsutaro Yanase, Yokosuka, Shizuoka Prefecture.

85. Edo *yakko,* a footman kite by Tokyo kite maker Teizo Hashimoto.

86. A hawk kite from Yokosuka, Shizuoka Prefecture. It has a three-dimensional head, only one bridle string, and flies easily and well. Falconry was a favorite sport of Ieyasu, the first Tokugawa military dictator, who lived in Shizuoka as a child and in his old age. Brown hawks, called *tobi,* like the one in this design are still seen in Shizuoka skies, as are hawk kites. By Matsutaro Yanase.

87. *Aka chochin* kite. The *aka chochin* is a red paper lantern that is often hung at the entrance of a public drinking house. From Takamatsu, Kagawa Prefecture.

10

THE WORLD'S LARGEST KITE,
THE HOSHUBANA SHOWA O-DAKO

I HAD WRITTEN SEVERAL LETTERS trying to find someone who was familiar with Japan's largest kite. Strangely enough, the kite I was looking for was not well known in its home country, and I had collected very little information about it by the time I arrived there. Most Japanese, I discovered, were only vaguely aware of its existence. My letters were finally directed to the little village of Hoshubana, Showa district, Saitama Prefecture, where the kite is made and flown. A reply from officials of the O-dako Association said, "It is very difficult to explain the giant kites by letter or over the telephone. Would you please come and visit our village?"

With this invitation to meet with the association, I was given detailed travel instructions. The complicated travel route explained in part why knowledge of the giant kites of Japan remains relatively regional. Another reason is that Hoshubana is such a tiny village that it does not appear on many maps.

Less than one hour north of congested Tokyo, the train carried my friend Munakata and me through lush green flatlands. Land is not wasted in Japan; rice is grown wherever there is available space: on tiny irregular-shaped plots of land, and even on mountain slopes, where the paddies are terraced. But here the landscape was unusually open and uncluttered. At our destination, broad plains of rice plants that moved gently in the breeze stretched clear to the horizon, a sight rare in mountainous, overcrowded Japan. From the village of Hoshubana, farm buildings far across the fields were visible, their thatch roofs protruding above two-story hedge fences. Threading through the green expanse of the plain was the Edogawa River, its high, grass-covered, sloping banks prominent against the skyline. Where the river skirts the village, the villagers have made its banks their kite-flying ground.

It was spring when we paid our visit. The plain was quietly beautiful, serene in its delicate new greenness. The appeal of the expansive farmland, virtually unbroken as it stretched toward the horizon, could not help but move anyone who has experienced the congestion of not only Tokyo but so much of Japan.

We ignored the few signs of aspiring modernity in the village and gave our full attention to the distinctive unpainted wooden architecture that remained from old Japan, buildings polished smooth where hands have rested or feet trod, others made dry and rough-textured by years of wind and dust. Few towns wish to be thought old-fashioned, but the look of Hoshubana was truly old-fashioned—in the best sense of the term. The old buildings were in such a state of good repair that the village had a restored but lived-in look, preserved and at the same time being put to the best possible use, that of human habitation.

We were met at the bus stop by three very ordinary-looking townsmen. One was the proprietor of a watch shop, the second the owner of a restaurant that specialized in eel, the local delicacy, and the third an employee of the village. Two of the men were in their fifties, one perhaps in his mid-sixties.

When the formalities were completed, we immediately fell into conversation about o-dako. Our hosts introduced themselves as three of the four officers of their group, an association that included 140 members. A brisk walk quickly brought us to the home of Mr. Ogawa, the restaurant owner, and there we were invited to sit down in a Western-style dining room. While we enjoyed the grilled eel served by Mr. Ogawa, the other two men, Masanobu Osato and Kazuo Akiyama, spoke of their long affiliation with the O-dako Association.

"About two hundred and sixty years ago," Akiyama began, "an itinerant Buddhist priest called Joshin stopped in this district. Joshin brought us an intriguing idea, one unfamiliar to our small farming community although fashionable in other parts of Japan. He said that kite flying was a means of divining the forthcoming year's silkworm production."

"Silk, at that time, was as important as rice," Osato added.

Priests such as Joshin, on pilgrimages to temples across Japan, supported themselves by various means, I later learned. Some performed Buddhist services for communities without priests while others were craftsmen. The pilgrimages they made, often begun in early youth, were sometimes not completed until old age. Villagers welcomed a traveling priest, and their hospitality helped to soften his hard life.

Joshin's divination method, considered even from a modern viewpoint, is not too far-fetched. For kites enter a region no human of that time had ever visited. This is the region of lightning and rainstorms, the wind or calm that had such an immediate effect on the delicate silkworms spinning their cocoons in the attics of Hoshubana houses far below. It seemed reasonable then to watch the actions of a flying kite to try to determine what the sky had in mind for the earth below. The principle is still followed today, for weathermen continue to send up instruments to gather information on the weather.

In the Hoshubana district, two and a half centuries ago, the words of the priest Joshin were convincing. The year following his visit, old documents tell us, some twenty or thirty kites were being flown.

The Hoshubana farmers were skillful in their profession. Their farms were large and their yields plentiful. Blessed with a "first-class river," as Osato called the Edogawa, they had an economical source of transportation to Edo, Japan's largest consumer. All factors combined to make the farmers of Hoshubana rich.

Today, however, with a population of a little over 2,000, it is by Japanese standards hardly more than a crossroads. In 1923 the Great Kanto Earthquake, which destroyed much of Tokyo, helped accelerate the decline of the river's importance as a commercial waterway. Then, about twenty-five years ago, a flood changed the river's path. Modern flood-control procedures compelled a broadening of the river and other changes to be made upstream, so that today the wide bed of the Edogawa where it passes Hoshubana is generally dry for long periods of time. Water is diverted all along its course for irrigation and into reservoirs that store drinking water for Tokyo. As a consequence, Hoshubana has come down in the world and is today a quiet rural backwater.

The O-dako Association officers regretted the passing of the era when Hoshubana was gay and lively and influential. "When the river was active," Osato recalled with sadness, "there were many good times here. Our town had many permanent geisha and there were many evenings of happiness. Everyone tasted rice and pleasure."

"Yes, and we have rice now," Akiyama added, "but I like kites better than rice! More than anything else!" With that the nostalgic mood was dispelled, and we went on to speak of little else but kites.

The kites that forecast the weather, the men told me, began to double as celebration kites for firstborn male children. Since the community was prosperous, the size of the kites grew larger as families began to use them as public announcements of a child's birth. At one time, kites were used for fighting. But perhaps because those who flew kites had no underlying reasons for discontent or because the big kites were simply too dangerous for that sport, kite fighting did not take hold in Hoshubana. Instead, the village tended to enjoy the community effort required in flying larger kites. The size of the kites was gradually increased. At the beginning of the Meiji era, around 1868, the Hoshubana kites were only half as large as the kites used today, the present dimensions being set twenty years later.

The giant kite of today is forty-eight by thirty-six feet—almost the size of the floor of a hundred-mat house, which was the actual basis for determining the kite's dimensions. It weighs around 1,750 pounds. Fifteen or so hundred-pound bags of rice are used as an anchor for it while it is being flown. The kite's bones are of bamboo. Its skin is made of 1,500 sheets of specially made paper that have been pasted together. The paper, called *nishi no uchi,* is only slightly heavier than ordinary paper, a tribute to the remarkable strength of Japan's unique handmade papers. Two hundred bridle lines, each a hundred feet long, are tied at regular intervals to the face of the kite. The flying line used, depending on wind conditions, will be 1,500 to 3,000 feet long. Two giant kites are flown simultaneously by two teams of flyers as part of the Hoshubana Showa Boys' Day O-dako Festival, a celebration held on the third and fifth of each May.

Akiyama, the district representative of one of the teams, described the festival for us. "On each kite are drawn two Japanese characters. When the two kites are flown together, the four characters complete one thought. In recent years, the messages, which are decided upon by the kite association members, have commemorated such national or regional anniversaries and events as Expo '70 and the hundredth anniversary of the Meiji Restoration."

At least one of the giant kites has flown on either of the two days of the festival since their first appearance nearly a century ago. Despite the unpredictability of the wind, the kites have performed remarkably well, a feat that gives the flyers no small measure of pride. Flying the kite can be dangerous, as was proved a few years ago. Although no one can recall a serious accident having occurred in the past, in 1971 a man was killed when a sudden gust of wind sent the kite whose tail he was holding sixty feet into the air. The kite fell seconds later, fatally injuring the flyer. The team whose kite had brought on the unfortunate death withdrew from the festival, and the other team flew a newly painted kite bearing four characters instead of the usual two.

In addition to the giant kites, two others half their size are flown. On these are written the names of the year's firstborn males. While the kites are being flown, the association officials make personal visits to the parents' homes and present them with gifts of fruit and small mementos. The new parents will in turn serve them sakè and donate money to help pay the costs of building the big kites.

To construct and fly these kites, the officials told us, the efforts of virtually the entire community are required. At least one person from each family contributes time, and all the helpers work under the supervision of the kite association. Two giant kites are made, each taking one month for completion. If a kite is broken on the first day of flying, a frantic period of work ensues in order to repair the kite or make a new one. When necessary, all the members of the kite association will work all night and the next day and night to prepare a new kite by the fifth of May.

The characters drawn on the o-dako kites are over twenty feet high. I had assumed that they would be drawn in outline, then patiently filled in with color, as is done with the kites made in Shirone and Hamamatsu. But this is not the case. The 1,500 sheets of paper, all pasted together, are laid out on the playground of the Hoshubana school. Then the letters are painted full size by a sixty-one-year-old calligraphy master, Soko Nakamura.

Akiyama described the lettering task: "The calligraphy master is a small man. His right arm, which never grew properly, dangles uselessly at his side, so that he works only with his left. When he is ready to paint the giant kite, he steps gingerly out onto the white paper carrying a huge dry brush. Its bristles are two-and-a-half feet long, its diameter a foot and a half across. He grips the mammoth brush with his good hand, the handle tucked under his useless arm, and stands for a while envisioning the placement of the design on the large expanse of pure white. His assistants place buckets of ink close by him as he contemplates his task. When he is ready, he loads the great brush with ink, carefully lifts it out of the bucket, and immediately swirls it down onto the paper, pushing and kicking it with his legs to make it move in wide strokes. At times, his assistants help him move the brush as he guides it along its path, gripping it against his whole body."

After the calligrapher has finished, there is still much to be done before the kite is ready for flying. The paper must be laid over the bamboo bones and its edges folded and pasted over the bones along the perimeter. Two hundred bridles are then passed through the paper and tied to the latticelike bamboo framework. Other ropes are tied at regular intervals along one side of the back, and are then drawn tautly across to the opposite side where they are tied fast. These are the lines that bow the kite, tightly at the top, slightly less toward the bottom, a method commonly used to help improve flight.

In preparation for transporting the kite, the bridles are temporarily chain-stitched together and tied with easily releasable knots that will keep the great mass from tangling. The kite is carried to a scaffold large enough to hold it upright along its length, and strong enough to hold the weight of the men perched at the top, who pull the kite up off the ground and tie it securely to the scaffold. When the kite is firmly attached, all two hundred bridle lines are then pulled away from the curved surface to a precisely centered point where they are all brought together and attached to the single flying line (Plates 97–100). This adjustment is one of the most crucial, for it determines whether or not the kite will fly straight up or fall immediately to the side. Additionally, the bridle lines help the kite retain a properly curved face when hit by the wind.

Now the Hoshubana o-dako is ready for flight. But before it is taken down from the scaffold, the fifty team members who will fly it are joined by senior members of the association and a Shinto priest, who gives his blessing. They pose stiffly at the base of the kite for the de rigeur photo-taking, an occasion too serious to be marred by smiling faces (Plate 101).

By this time there are 30,000 spectators (on the second day there will be 70,000) impatiently waiting to see the kites fly. The kite association members and flyers are attired in a special costume of white slacks and celebration *happi* coats. The spectators stand or sit in small groups scattered all along the riverbed and banks. Many women will carry parasols to protect themselves from the sun, while baseball caps are favored by boys and men. Depending upon wind conditions, the kites are flown sometime between one and three in the afternoon.

Official team members, with the help of many ten- to-twelve-year old children, lift the long bundles of bridle lines. Twenty to thirty other men surround the kite, lift it up, and holding it over their heads, follow the bridle carriers, who lead the team up the sloping bank on the Saitama Prefecture side of the Edogawa.

The bridle lines are carefully laid out in long lines on the wide path at the top of the bank. The fifty-man team divides itself into three groups, each group moving into position along the flying line. The men stationed at the kite itself take up thirty-foot-long bamboo poles and lift the kite into a vertical position. Standing tall as it now is, the kite is in a dangerous position, its fragility exposed to every stray gust. In the brief space between the upending of the kite and its takeoff, its great weight causes it to sag slightly at the corners.

Until this moment, all the preparations for flight have been painstakingly slow and cautious. But now is the time when quickly coordinated actions are essential. The wind pushes a warning shudder across the kite's face as the bridle lines snap taut. When the men supporting the kite with the long poles suddenly run out of the way, the wind pushes it backward and the slack flying line tightens, putting a growing strain on the flyers positioned along the flying line who dig in their heels to hold back the lifting line. Those nearest the kite feel themselves growing lighter as the rising line pulls them upward. The man responsible for balancing the kite until the last second now runs out of the way and throws himself flat on the ground as the kite overtakes him, skims the ground, and starts its ascent. The loud ringing of a gong sends all three groups of linemen running into the slight wind, pulling the kite after them. Their speed increases as they run diagonally down the sloping river bank and onto its dry bed (Plates 97–100).

The team nearest the kite drops the flying line and rushes to regroup behind the last team, and here they are followed by the second team and then the third. By alternating positions in this way, the strain, which is greatest on those nearest the kite, is relieved, while at the same time, more line is let out so that the kite can continue to move upward into the sky.

The kite is up now, a commanding presence that draws an admiring cheer from the spectators. But so absorbed in the harmony of their efforts are the flyers that they seem almost indifferent to the spectators and their concerns. They grit their teeth and rivet their eyes to the giant apparition they are loosing into the skies while across their faces a play of emotions—mostly strain, but also excitement, satisfaction, joy, and relief—marks the event. Curiously, although all of them have been certain of success, there is also an air of disbelief about them, a bit of innocent wonder, as though they had participated in the creation of a minor miracle.

Almost anticlimactically, from farther down the riverbed the second kite rises to join the first, capping the events of the day.

THE KITE FLYING finished for another year, we slowly made our way back to where we could catch a Tokyo-bound bus. Along the way we stopped at a Buddhist temple. Our hosts were still on the lookout for kite lore that might interest us. They took us to the temple veranda and pointed beneath it to the place where the bones of the village kites were stored between the annual festivals. A funeral service was in progress, and the scent of burning incense filled the air. By the time we reached the bus stop, we were talked out about the events of the day. The crowd of spectators was already gone and the village, like a housewife who has seen company off, had slipped back to its everyday look.

A funeral gong sounded, and then there was only the silence of the dusty main street. I was thinking of how pleasant it would be to live in Hoshubana. The people we had met and the village itself represent the best of old Japan. And nearby is Tokyo, archetype of new Japan, and yet not without a distinctive appeal. It was a pleasing thought, that of drawing on the best of the old and the new for inspiration. And every year there would be two very special days to look forward to, those days when the great Hoshubana kites rise in splendor over the green plains.

11

BAMBOO AND PAPER

THE KITE MAKER OF JAPAN works intimately with two of his country's most remarkable assets, bamboo and paper. Without their ready availability and suitability, he no doubt would have already embraced plastic for his modern kites. The Japanese kite, however, is virtually synonymous with bamboo and paper. It is a tribute to the beauty and utilitarian qualities of these materials that they continue to enhance daily life in Japan in so many ways. I often wonder what America would be like today if it had been blessed with Japan's bamboo and paper. A little more like Japan, I would guess, and richer for it.

ONE DAY, while climbing the side of a gently sloping mountain covered with bamboo, the stillness around me was broken by the dry, rustling noise of leaves far overhead. As the wind, at first not noticeable in the middle of the grove, increased, the tall bamboo responded. The thirty-foot-high stems came alive, whipping back and forth in the wind, the limbs and leaves of each plant locked together in a slow and graceful dance. Within the grove it was beautiful, and a little awesome.

The sight of a bamboo grove from a bus or train window immediately makes clear why so many Japanese (as well as Korean and Chinese) artists have chosen to portray this plant. Bamboo groves, both cultivated and wild, add greatly to the natural beauty of the Japanese landscape. Without much effort I can imagine a nature lover devoting his life to two great growing things, the giant redwoods of America's West Coast and the thin, lithe bamboo.

Bamboo appears everywhere in daily life in Japan, and the Western visitor is always astonished at the variety of uses to which it can be put. The list is nearly endless: There is the unadorned bamboo leaf containing sweet amber syrup that has been hardened into a patty, the leaf folded over to form a candy wrapper; the *shakuhachi*, a bamboo flute whose deep voice to me is like the rush of an awesome wind sweeping through deep caverns; the long, narrow laminated bow (with an inner core of oak or other hardwood) and its arrows, equipment with which the Japanese archer is trained to identify so closely that all, including the target, become one; and the bamboo handle of an artist's brush. There are also woven baskets of innumerable shapes and sizes, bamboo garden fences, floors or walls of houses, cooking spoons, chopsticks, ladders, rakes, toys, blinds, fans, tea whisks, umbrellas, kites. And each article, made with a high degree of skill and aesthetic sensitivity, enriches its user's life. Why bamboo was chosen for these objects is simple, for few other common materials so harmoniously blend beauty and utility.

Bamboo is suitable for kites in several ways: in long, thin strips it is remarkably strong, and its flexibility allows a kite to adjust to changes in the wind. It is also inexpensive and readily available. Kite makers have favorite locations from which they obtain their bamboo. Generally the groves are located relatively near the kite maker's workshop, although he will choose stems from a great many sources within his district. There are favored times for cutting the bamboo that will be used for making kite bones, and different ideas about the time required for the bamboo to dry, these factors being subject to regional, personal, and traditional preferences. The most commonly preferred time for cutting is in the autumn, before the bamboo is liable to be attacked by insects. Proper seasoning may take from six months to as long as two or three years. Although some kite makers go to the groves and cut their own bamboo, most place orders for bones that have been properly seasoned with dealers who are expert in their profession and deal exclusively in bamboo.

The bamboo used in the arts undergoes treatment to protect it from insects and to help it resist the mold that is always a problem in a climate as humid as Japan's. One method of treatment is to heat the bamboo by passing it through a flame; another is to boil the bamboo, generally in a soda solution. Watanabe, the Shirone kite maker, believes heating reduces the bamboo's strength and flexibility, although some heating is necessary to remove the oil which, he says, "is like sugar to some insects." He himself prefers the boiling soda solution to eliminate this appeal.

The bamboo bones appear on the reverse side of a kite, a relatively inconspicuous position. Usually hidden from view, there is little motivation for the kite maker to expend his time and energy exploring their aesthetic potential. The very word "bone" implies that their purpose is primarily structural. Bones may reveal a certain simple beauty, although any conscious striving for visual effect in this area is minimal. Not all Japanese kite makers, however, share this sentiment. Two kite types—the Nagasaki hata and the kites fashioned by Yanase, of Yokosuka—show a refinement far exceeding functional requirements. I don't know why this is so; perhaps the artists who make these kites simply feel the urge to carry design further than the other kite makers.

LIKE SO MANY other materials in Japan, paper too has come in for many hundreds of years of artistic consideration. At one period of the country's history, the paper on which a poem was written was as significant as the poem itself. A thousand years ago there were whole towns actively engaged in making paper. Such towns still exist, but there were also many farming villages which then, as they do today, made paper to earn extra income during the winter. At present, roughly half of Japan's farmers must supplement their incomes with winter jobs. Although a large percentage of winter employment is provided by construction companies, some farmers continue to work at such cottage industries as paper making.

The farmer who makes paper may interrupt his work at any point to perform other chores in the home and the fields. For both farmer and professional, sun, wind, and running water are necessary. And because nature is not always predictable, it too may interrupt the process of paper making. These factors contribute day by day, month by month, and year by year to the subtle variations in color and texture of handmade paper. A keen sensitivity to the nuances of weather, growing cycles, purity of water, quality of plants, duration of a snowfall, and temperature is required. This is acquired over generations of living close to nature.

The romantic ideas associated with paper become less so when one realizes the amount of demanding physical work that goes into its making. Much of the paper maker's time is spent outdoors in the snow. Enduring the cold is the most difficult but not the only hardship. The paper maker works long hours, about ten a day, with hands in icy water, taking no vacations, and making just enough money to exist on. Constant reminders of the consequences of this devotion are chilblains, permanent cold sores, painful wounds, and stiffness and swelling that lasts all year round. The paper maker who continues to work under these circumstances may be likened to an artist who in pursuit of art is oblivious to harsh conditions. It takes ten years to learn this art, and today it is largely practiced by women, for the men of a paper-making family handle the business transactions.

I have heard of only one kite maker who makes his own paper. There may be others, but most Japanese kite makers rely on the professional paper maker. Paper is made to order specifically for a particular kite artist or for one of the big festival kites, although there is little to distinguish this kind from ordinary handmade paper. There are a great many varieties of handmade paper, however, made for many different purposes. Kite paper (and umbrella paper) is approximately the weight of good bond paper. In comparison with other papers, it is noticeably sturdier because its fibers are longer and therefore stronger. Paper used for shoji, paper-covered sliding doors, is slightly thinner than kite paper, and that used for woodblock printing can be quite heavy (postcard weight); calligraphy paper is considerably thinner, close to an onionskin weight. All the Japanese handmade papers are noticeably softer than Western papers, and it is easy to mistake many varieties for cloth. In fact, paper has long been used for making some articles of dress.

Japanese handmade paper has several distinctive qualities particularly appropriate to kites. One is its economy. Another is its extraordinary strength. Machine-made paper can be used only to make small kites because Japanese kites, particularly large ones, endure stresses that kites using machine-made paper of a similar weight cannot take. In the West, kites o comparable size had to be covered in cloth. The Japanese could have used cloth, of course; but if they had, we would have been left with a considerably different art. Lanterns have been made with silk covers, but I believe there is little doubt as to the superiority of paper. Not the least of the qualities of paper is its beauty.

Paper was introduced into Japan by a Korean priest known as Doncho around the year 610. The paper-making process he brought with him had originated in China. Doncho's paper was brittle, but two hundred years later Japan's paper makers developed a superior paper, for which there was a great demand in China. Over the centuries further improvements resulted in the many varieties of paper now distinctly Japanese.

At first, paper was used exclusively by the aristocracy; the common man, even if he had been literate, could not have afforded it. One example of early uses of paper was the widespread copying of Buddhist sutras. These texts from the Buddhist scriptures were often written in gold and silver on thick blue paper. Light and dark gray sheets of paper made from the recycled letters of departed loved ones were also used for sutra copying. By the middle of the fourteenth century, many varieties of paper were being produced throughout Japan. Henceforth, it was available to the masses and used in a great number of ways: paper for shoji and umbrellas was made in virtually every district, as well as heavy paper for clothing. Japanese handmade paper was exported in large quantities until the Tokugawa government began to enforce a policy of national isolation in the early years of the seventeenth century. With the end of the Tokugawa regime, in 1868, and the reopening of the country to trade, the exportation of paper was resumed. At this time, Western paper-making machinery was introduced to meet growing demands. But today, even though most Japanese paper is machine-made, it is still the handmade variety that one associates with Japan.

Japanese handmade paper is called washi. Westerners have come to refer to it as "rice paper," which is an unfortunate misnomer. There is nothing remotely connected with rice in any Eastern handmade paper. The misnomer is generally attributed to the English and is thought to have come from guesses as to how the substance was made.

Put simply, the paper-making process involves breaking vegetable matter into fibers, floating these in water, and then allowing them to settle on a porous screen so that a thin sheet of paper is formed. The following paragraphs describe an amalgamation of a variety of methods, materials, and equipment used in Japanese paper making today.

There are several paper fibers in popular use. The *kozo* tree, a type of mulberry, is the most important source. Noted for its strength, kozo fiber has traditionally been used for making kite paper. In two years its shoots are ready for collecting. In the autumn, when the leaves have fallen, the shoots are cut back to the ground, leaving a stump from which next year's growth will sprout (the tree will produce this way for twenty years). The kozo grows wild, but because it is always threatened with extermination by rice paddies and buildings climbing farther and farther up mountain slopes, it is also cultivated. The paper maker must often depend on kozo farms to supply him with this material.

The one- to two-foot-long kozo shoots are placed in a large iron kettle over which is set a larger wooden tub. The shoots are boiled for several hours until the outer bark softens and peels easily. The outermost layers, including the bark, are peeled into long strips while still warm, then draped over a pole to dry in the sun and wind. When they have dried they are bundled and stored, generally until winter, or until a time convenient for paper making.

At the next stage, the long strands of bark are separated, again hung on poles, and this time placed in streams to be cleaned and softened by running water. When it is soft enough, the black outer bark is scraped away with a knife, leaving strips of the white layer. This white inner bark is the portion of the kozo that forms the basis of paper. It is washed in the stream and dried in the sun for three or four days to rid it of any remaining gummy residue (Plates 103–4).

The white inner bark is then boiled in a large cauldron containing a soda ash solution. The mass is constantly stirred, then covered and left to steam to rid it of all that is non-cellulose. In the process, this too is softened and partially bleached. The boiled bark is put into a bamboo basket and returned to the stream for the last time. The flowing water of the stream, acting as a natural bleaching agent, helps to remove impurities.

It is usually the older women who work by hand removing pieces of bark or other impurities (Plate 105). If this task is done in winter, as it most frequently is, it is very unpleasant, if not truly painful work. (I have heard it said that the appeal of Japan's famous hot springs for rural people was the relief the waters provided from the ills resulting from paper making.) Unfortunately for the paper maker, the icy coldness of a mountain stream in winter is inescapable, since optimum blending of the natural ingredients occurs at cold temperatures. In addition, the pure mountain stream is free of minerals that might discolor and spot the paper.

The kozo is now snow white, and this doughlike mass is kneaded into cantaloupe-size balls. The final step in the preparation of the kozo is to break the fibers down and separate them into the desired lengths. In the recent past, wooden sticks were employed, but today machines are generally used. These fibers remain visible in all Japanese handmade paper, adding considerably to its distinctive beauty.

One more plant figures in paper making. This is the *tororo,* a type of yam from which is obtained a material that helps the fibers float uniformly in the solution and prevents the sheets of paper from sticking together when they are stacked.

The remaining steps in paper making involve simple materials. If one is at all familiar with the paper-making process, there is a tendency to associate paper making with this final stage and forget the many difficult procedures involved up to this point. The major reason for the appeal of the final stages is that this is when tonality and texture are determined and the actual sheet of paper first appears.

The necessary equipment for paper making consists of a large rectangular wooden tub in which the ingredients are whipped together, a finely woven bamboo screen, and the paper maker's (here, too, almost invariably a woman's) two strong arms. The screen is dipped into the thick, milky liquid, and with a practiced rocking motion called scooping, the paper maker slushes the proper amount of liquid carefully from front to back. The kozo fibers settle evenly on the screen, while the water escapes through the mesh (Plate 106).

The bamboo screen is then removed from its rigid frame, and the fresh paper that has settled out onto the screen is transferred to a wooden platform. The sheets of wet paper are stacked one on top of the next. Up to six hundred sheets of paper a day may be made in this fashion. Each one will be unique, yielding slight variations to the observant eye.

The stack is left standing overnight. The next day, excess water is pressed out of the sheets. The tororo root has done its job of preventing the sheets from adhering to one another. One by one the sheets are removed, flattened out with a brush on a long, smooth pine plank, and left to dry in the sun (Plate 107). One might think that all paper would be of reasonably uniform thickness, even handmade paper. This is not so, and considerable skill is needed to produce a sheet of the commonest paper.

Sukey Hughes, an American studying under the master paper maker Ichibei Iwano (who has been designated a Living National Treasure by the Japanese government), gave me this description of present-day paper-making villages: "What a difference there is among paper-making towns: some so poor and pathetic, cobwebs in the corners, dust falling into the vats, and the old man at work in the musty sunlight that is strained by the fiber-encrusted window probably makes interesting paper, though likely it is not of high quality—too much clay added for weight, or perhaps he's used straw in it.

"By contrast, take a village such as Kurodani in Kyoto Prefecture: deep green hills bathed in sunlight, gay children playing, and women gossiping as they pass along the small lane near the village river. The women have been beating pulp and are now bringing it home. A small station wagon chugs up the lane selling fish and bean curds to women too busy to leave their work to go shopping. The women's faces are open, ruddy, and healthy, though a little tiredness shows through from behind their eyes. Their work never ends: some scoop from nine in the morning to nine or eleven at night. Their husbands, who work at salaried jobs, drive to work in cars or on motorcycles. These days the children all leave home after graduation to work in urban centers like Tokyo and Kyoto. No one is learning paper making. It's too tough. But the people are so friendly, frank, hearty, even happy. Everywhere there is paper making: old women washing bark in the stream or hanging it to dry while children play in nearby bamboo groves. The paper made here is honest, crisp, fresh, and strong. In the fall and winter there are orange-colored persimmons on the trees; in spring, plum and cherry blossoms. The shrines are often dedicated to a local god of paper.

"Walking along the street of a paper-making village you can hear the distinctive sloshing of water in the frame screen, a definite rhythm, almost music. Someone may even be up scooping until midnight. The sound joins the rushing of the river. Bits of fiber and black bark stick to the windows, to people's hands, and under their fingernails. The acrid smell of alkali from fibers being boiled hangs in the air, and a vegetable odor permeates the room when the paper is scooped.

"Women walk about the village in white aprons. Everywhere natural materials are employed, like the horsehair brush used to flatten the paper on long wood boards for drying, or the leaf used to smooth down the corner of a drying sheet. Split bamboo pipes channel water into a building from a nearby stream; great stones weigh down stacks of wet paper.

A piece of kozo bark is used as an emergency rope. A stack of freshly cut paper is rolled and then bound with a small strip of twisted paper. Doors and windows are covered with fine handmade paper. Such sights, sounds, and smells of the paper-making village never fail to refresh my spirit."

The papers made in such villages come in a great number of patterns, colors, and transparencies, and vary according to their texture and thickness. They are all perfectly suited to a great variety of purposes: shoji; fans; lanterns; materials upon which a poem, calligraphy, or painting is done; wrapping paper; or kite paper. The paper usually comes to life when light filters through it, exposing the texture and arrangement of the fibers.

At first, while it was still rare, handmade paper enjoyed the highest esteem. And it is still far from being taken for granted. In ancient times a sheet of paper was counted as a fine gift, and this still holds true in modern Japan. Gift receiving is an ever-pleasant activity for a visitor to Japan. My first gift there was a sheet of paper, given to me by my friend Kuni-yoshi Munakata on the occasion of our first meeting. Made by his wife's family in Shikoku many years before, it was a deep brown color, speckled with shades of gray and tan, and rolled and tied with a ribbon. Although it may sound too sentimental to say so in modern times, a gift like this is something to be cherished.

The beauty ascribed to the Japanese kite cannot be separated from the beauty of the paper from which it is created. In traditional Japan, poetry is inseparable from the gesture in the poet's calligraphy, and the calligraphy is inseparable from the paper's surface. These qualities are shared by the Japanese kite.

12

TWO SCULPTORS WHO MAKE KITES: TSUTOMU HIROI AND TAL STREETER

Enjoying kites is not the special province of artists. Nearly every adult has made or flown at least one kite in his lifetime. It is another thing, however, to enjoy kites as fine art, and still another to continue to make and fly them through adulthood, for normally we associate kites with the child's world. Making and flying kites may seem even more anachronistic now, with our skies full of gigantic jet aircraft, supersonic planes, satellites, and spaceships, than it did in times past. The sky is the same of course, but the things we send into it, with their great noises and velocities, seem to diminish the kite's importance. The kite need not be demeaned by these giants, however, for there is little that is man-made and flies that can rival the fragile beauty of a kite dancing in air.

Both Tsutomu Hiroi and I deeply enjoy kites. And both of us are primarily sculptors, working with the modern materials and ideas of contemporary sculpture. Kites, seen in the totality of my own sculpture, emerge as a movement toward a softer poetry; for Hiroi they represent a lifelong love of things that fly.

TSUTOMU HIROI'S KITES

I arrived at Hiroi's suburban Tokyo home for a visit late one night. At seven o'clock the next morning a muffled roar in the distance gently brought me awake. I sleepily considered the possibility of an explosion somewhere far off, but quickly came fully awake as the roar increased in intensity and the window glass began to rattle with an unnerving clatter. The house started to shake vigorously as the first wave of an earthquake struck it frontally and the second wave, without a pause, struck sideways. Hiroi and I shouted questions at each other in the excitement and creaking of the wooden frame house. I barely had the wits to run to the doubtful safety of the bedroom doorway where Hiroi already stood. In less than a minute from start to finish, the earthquake subsided, the earth stopped trembling, the rumble died away, and all in the house was as quiet as before. Hiroi, with the indifference gained from similar experiences, immediately climbed back into bed. But sleep was out of the question for me, and I went downstairs, shaken wide-awake by my first experience with earthquakes.

Later, on the way to Tokyo Gakugei University, where Hiroi has an office and studio, he told me that his wife calls the small, round vase that fell on the floor during the quake their "earthquake barometer." Sometimes they find it on the floor upon their return home, and they know that an earthquake has occurred. "When the vase is finally broken," he said, "it will be due to a bad one." He jokingly referred to that morning's quake as "the wake-up earthquake."

Hiroi has visited the United States several times. He taught sculpture, design, and kite making at California College of Arts and Crafts, Ohio State University, and the University of Denver. He has worked with sculptor Isamu Noguchi on several projects, one an international competition in New Delhi. Their team, whose members were Noguchi, Hiroi, and two architects, Katsumi Komuro and Yozo Shibata, won fourth place with a design of an 80-foot-high bell tower. The blueprints of one of Hiroi's early proposals to the group showed me that he has the ability to move easily beyond the traditional limitations of "what sculpture should be." His design was of a straightforward 900-foot-high steel radio-television tower to be used for "the broadcast of Buddha."

On one of his trips to the United States he spent three months working in Noguchi's studio in New York City. When Noguchi comes to Japan, he often works with Hiroi. On an earlier visit they worked with traditional paper lantern craftsmen in Gifu, trying to learn how to solve the problems of manufacturing Noguchi's modern Akari paper lanterns. Hiroi does designs for several traditional and modern Japanese dance groups and, like Noguchi, has designed costumes and props for the Martha Graham Dance Company.

Hiroi and I share an enthusiasm for Noguchi and his work, and for the work of Constantin Brancusi. Many years ago when Noguchi was a young sculptor, he worked for a year with Brancusi in Paris. I mentioned to Hiroi that Noguchi once told me he had learned how to sweep a floor while working for Brancusi. Brancusi, Noguchi said, kept his studio meticulously clean. Hiroi laughed when he saw me glance around his studio. "Yes," he said, "I wish I, in turn, had learned that art from Noguchi." The large room we were in, his office and studio, was not dirty, but unbelievably cluttered. There were literally hundreds of kites, either hanging from the ceiling or stacked on the floor. There were old model airplanes on shelves, notebooks, paper models of sculptures, and the works themselves stacked in corners and on stands among the kites.

Hiroi's versatile mind leads him in many directions, as the state of his studio shows. But he can also be methodical when the occasion requires. During our first talk, for instance, he referred frequently to a penciled chart on which he had clearly outlined his sculptures with their dates of inception and completion. He quickly sketched another simple chart which showed that though there is much in common among the four of us, neither Noguchi nor Brancusi had made kites—"but perhaps Noguchi will yet," he added. Hiroi has shown his sculpture in Japan's museums for nearly twenty years. In 1969 he sent kites to the annual exhibition of painting and sculpture held at the Tokyo National Museum of Modern Art. "That was the first time I said publicly that kites are sculpture," he commented.

"Let me tell you something about myself," he once offered. "When I was ten, children liked airplanes very much, for they were rarely seen over Japan. We shouted 'Airplane!' whenever one appeared and sometimes we were thrilled by actually seeing the pilot inside the cockpit.

"I liked anything that flew, insects and butterflies, and particularly pigeons. When I was in primary school, I used to pass a bird shop every day on my way to and from school. I became keenly interested in the eggs one pigeon laid and one day I told the shopkeeper that when they hatched, I would like to buy her squabs. Each day I went to the shop to look at the pigeon's eggs. In seventeen days the eggs hatched, one male and one female, as is nearly always the case. Shortly after that I bought the tiny squabs and took them home. From then on, until I was a university student, I raised thirty pigeons all together.

"At that time I also made model airplanes of all sizes and descriptions, as well as kites. Everything connected with flying fascinated me."

When he entered the university Hiroi wanted to study airplane design and engineering, but because there were no vacancies he enrolled in art courses.

"While at the university I flew gliders, and once I went up in a training fighter. We were doing all kinds of rolls and turns, and although the Gs hitting my face were painful, I was completely thrilled. Much later, Masayuki Nagare, a sculptor who had flown Zeros, several other artists, and I formed the Air-Space Group. We went up in a rented Cessna to take photographs, draw, and make notes. Later, we made sculpture and paintings based on what we observed and felt. These were exhibited around 1954 or 1955.

"When I made an airplanelike kite, a three-dimensional cubic kite, for the first time some thirty years ago, I was thrilled by its wonderful performance. Unlike an ordinary kite, it ascended high into the air as the wind velocity increased, riding above the wind rather than against it.

"As a child, I used to take my pigeons to the roof in the evening. I enjoyed watching them circling in the sky above. Often I would send my kites up with them. The roof was slightly peaked in the middle and it was difficult to stand on the sloping sides, and nearly impossible to run there. It was on that roof that I learned to fly kites without running. It's hard to describe this method, but it involves an awareness of the feel of the wind, its direction, and the characteristics of the kite. In time, anyone can develop his own techniques. The amateur usually keeps his hands high above his head, trying in this way to keep the kite that much higher off the ground. But, because the string must be let out and pulled in quickly, I keep my hands as low as possible, with the string close to the ground so that it doesn't get all mixed up like a bunch of wet noodles."

Hiroi, now in his mid-forties, flies kites with apparent ease from the flat third-floor roof of his university building. We went there once with a few recently purchased Chinese kites and some of his own caterpillar-shaped kites (Plate 110). There was hardly any wind that day, but he flew all the kites so effortlessly that it seemed they didn't need any. He prepared to fly a tiny kite made of a thin sheet of plastic and two nonrigid bones by unwinding an extremely long string. On an adjacent roof, I held the little kite aloft. The kite left my hand and moved out at the end of 3,000 feet of thin fishing line. Hiroi was using a fishing reel for rapid winding and unwinding. He let the line out quickly in order to make the kite rise. The kite responded by tumbling over itself, but then Hiroi quickly reeled the line in and the kite righted itself, billowed out, and rose speedily. It was an impressive feat. An amateur, myself included, would not have gotten the kite to fly at all, let alone at the end of 3,000 feet of string.

His conversation bounded around animatedly as he was distracted in turn by my questions and by the little kite far above us. Once, when the kite flew out of sight, I told Hiroi I could no longer see it. He nodded and replied, "I can still see it fairly clearly. But I have better than average long-distance vision. Kite flying is good for the eyes, I believe."

He continued playing with the kite a bit and said, "I worry about airplanes when the kite flies this high," then thought for a moment about what he had said and added with a laugh, "But kites were first and the planes should say excuse me to them.

"I try to keep kite making alive in Japan by teaching about kites to as many children and their teachers as possible. Sometimes I teach a course called Sculpture: Design, and we make kites in the classroom all day long."

When I asked how his university colleagues felt about his kite flying, he replied, "I tell them I am not an expert on sculpture, but I can be one on kites. Of course they laugh. When they saw me once or twice on television discussing kites, I went up in their estimation a bit. At parties I'm pointed out and people say, with some awe in their voices, we saw him on television. The Japanese have a weakness for mass-media personalities."

The kite expert brought out a clear plastic raincoat with two long sticks running parallel about twenty inches apart along the back. "A raincoat kite," he explained. "I can wear this kite if it rains, and I can fly it as well. And to make it, I didn't cut the original raincoat at all!" He laughed delightedly over the raincoat turned kite. He put the raincoat on, then took it off and sent it soaring far up into the sky (Plates 108–9). It was a marvelous display of ingenuity, at once childlike and sophisticated.

"I am interested in the earth and the sky," he said, still busy with his flying raincoat. "The earth is heavy and is the more obviously sculptural, but the sky . . . it's hard to catch the sky."

In an article explaining the emotions of passionate kite flyers, he once wrote: "Those of us who love kite flying can hardly keep still when an agreeable wind blows: children coming from school rush to an open field to fly kites. It is very satisfying for us to look up at a kite floating in a fair wind against the blue sky, to feel man and sky linked by a thin string, to feel the wind through the vibrating string. And when he brings the kite in safely, the flyer feels the kite is some new creature come to life by having been filled full of fresh air."

Another time he said, "Flying kites is more relaxing than exhilarating for me." Which makes me think that perhaps Hiroi too partakes of Modegi's kite enlightenment.

TAL STREETER'S FLYING RED LINE

NEITHER HIROI NOR MYSELF, though we think of ourselves as sculptors first, is deeply concerned about whether or not kites should be considered fine art. Perhaps kites are unique enough after all to elude categorization—as does bamboo, which is neither tree nor grass but just bamboo.

Initially, I was attracted to a piece of string hanging in the sky connected to a scrap of paper and sticks on one end and a hand on the other. Gradually, kites began to tell me something about my steel sculptures, artworks that weigh tons. In time, paper and steel, earth and sky became inextricably joined in my art.

I had gone to Japan to make kites. The idea, a strange one to my friends in the art world, held more than a hint of enigma for me as well. I did not pretend to be able to predict the outcome of my search. Although I had often flown kites as a child, it was a pastime, without that ever-present enthusiasm that characterizes a true quest. Kite flying was a sometime thing, interrupted often and for long spells by more demanding preoccupations.

I made my first kite around the time of my ninth birthday. The sticks were scraps of pine, the paper a large, flattened-out brown paper bag. I had two full summers of fun with that kite; I seldom tired of sending it toward the Kansas sun, to whose intense heat I remained indifferent. I had other toys to play with, but the kite was a favorite from noon to sundown through that summer and the following one.

My father worked at the Boeing aircraft plant, where the B-29s used during World War II were manufactured. I was a fourth-grade student at the time, and our house was situated near the B-29 landing field, at the point where the big planes lined up with the airport runway and dropped out of the sky to land. My friends and I were oblivious to the destruction the planes represented. At night we often played outside in pitch blackness, and the suddenness of a bomber's brilliant lights flashing down from the sky added an enjoyable dimension to our games of hide-and-seek. Strangely enough, though I never forgot the big planes, it was not until I thought about writing this chapter that I remembered it was B-29s made at that plant that dropped the atomic bombs on Japan.

The Christmas between the two summers at our temporary wartime home was a milestone on the road to my becoming a sculptor. Hanging from the branches of that year's Christmas tree were many small packages, and underneath the tree was a still larger gift. All the gifts were for me. I had never gotten so many presents and couldn't imagine what they could be.

The first package contained a folding rule, the next a hammer, then a saw, a pair of pliers, and several other carpenter's tools. The big present turned out to be a wooden tool chest my father had made for me. All those gifts . . . but I was terribly disappointed. These weren't toys, I felt. In time, however, I grew away from that disappointment. My father taught me how to use the tools properly, and the idea of making things flowed uninterrupt-edly from that point to today. With the exception of that Christmas morning, I have ever since loved tools and making things.

Many years later, when I first lived in the countryside, just at the edge of New York City, I had occasion to fly a Japanese kite at a "kite-flying tree-climbing picnic" I gave for artist and gallery friends. I was flying a standard American kite which, lacking a tail, shuddered, jumped, and darted, virtually out of control. I put it aside for a little Japanese kite with open side pockets, and was amazed to see and feel it go straight up without the slightest hesitation and fly absolutely smoothly. In fact, it seemed to fly itself. Flying these two kites started me wondering whether the differences between them might point to broader implications about the differences between East and West.

Kites started coming back into my life about that time. After anxious and exhausting days spent in a studio or university, I often returned home, got a kite out of the garage, and, until the sun went down, flew it quietly from a nearby hill for a few hours of solitude. If I had a lot of string out, I sometimes tied the kite to a tree where it would fly for several days and and nights until the fragile string broke or the kite was pushed back to the ground. Kite flying, it occurred to me, is a way to stop time, to quieten anxieties, to eternalize the present moment. The pleasure of stopping time with a kite has been expressed by the Japanese poet Buson (in R. H. Blyth's *Haiku: Spring*):

> *Ikanobori*   A kite—
> *kino no sora no* in the same place
> *aridokoro*   in yesterday's sky!

In my mid-twenties and through my thirties the character of the sculpture I would make was becoming well established. Some elements were permanently in flux, but several major characteristics appeared to be relatively constant. One constant was linearity. Another was a sense of place—the environment in which the sculpture existed, I felt, was as im-portant as the work itself. The sculpture called attention not only to itself, but to the space around it. The space was not necessarily dictated by the precise locale of the sculpture; rather, it was related to perceptions of the earth as horizontally stable with the bowl of the sky overhead. My sculptures became very simple: straight lines and geometric angles. As often as not they were painted a deep red color. I called these works *Red Lines, Standing Red,* etc.

Ten years before this time, a child in a grade school art class taught by my wife had proudly shown me a drawing she had made, some frantic red crayon marks in the middle of a sheet of manila paper. She called it *Running Red*. Her insight has brought me closer to my own works, which have essentially become red entities, man-made objects left in the land-scape as a kind of marker of the presence of man. At the same time they call attention to their natural environments.

Sculpture, and painting as well, my own teachers said, keeps the eye moving around within its own boundaries, locked into its forms. It was correct, they cautioned, to rid the sculpture of anything that would send the eye out and away from the work itself. But I was happy to make objects that drew the eye away from the sculpture and led it right out into the landscape or sky. A philosopher-preacher-parapsychologist whom I admired volunteered the information that such sculpture acted as a kind of *koan*, the Zen answerless riddles that send the mind jumping off into insights greater than those available by means of traditional linear thinking. Such Zen-like sculpture existed as a means to an end, pointing away from itself to a broader nature rather than inward toward itself. Through my friend's patient explanations over a period of several years of the koan and Japanese thought, I found myself drawn to Japan, a country I quickly recognized was already existing in part within me. The exact relationship of the kites I thought of making to my sculpture was not clear to me, but I felt I could rely on intuition as the Zen trainee does on the koan: wherever it took me would be acceptable.

Part of nonlinear thought draws heavily on the emotional, the irrational (I subscribe to the view that the subconscious is a deeper rationality). Paradox is courted. There is paradox in the fact that I had worked all my adult life at welding heavy steel and then went to Japan to work with scissors cutting paper. In the United States, almost without interruption, I had cut metal by hand and with power machinery. The shrill screams and chatter of tearing metal made ear covers necessary. Dark goggles protected my eyes from blindness caused by the brilliant flashes and intense heart of oxy-acetylene or arc-welding equipment. Each day was filled with the cutting, bending, filing, and grinding of hard steel. And the powdered metal from the grinding wheel completely covered my hair and the pores of my skin with a silver-gray color by the end of a day's work. All day long I sweated and groaned as I lifted half-finished steel sculptures up into the air. I loved it.

In a short span of time, I found myself in Japan, where kneeling on a clean, resilient tatami mat, I was pinning down the thin slivers of bamboo I had split with a quick stroke of a small knife. I tied them together with cotton string to make the kite's form, then pasted on beautiful Japanese handmade paper. After the paste dried, I melted paraffin in a pan on the kitchen stove and painted thin lines of hot wax onto the paper surface to separate or contain the colors of the kite design. The final step, done out on the lawn under a hot sun, was to paint the "red line" in brilliant red dye. After a time, I found that I loved both steel and paper.

One of the steel sculptures I made in the United States, just prior to leaving for Japan, was a work called *Endless Column,* dedicated to Brancusi. The red line zigzagged up into the sky to a height of nearly seventy feet. The viewer's eye moved up from the base slowly, gathered speed toward the top, and finally sped off into the sky. The kites I made in Japan were named *Red Line in the Sky* and *Flying Red Line* (Plates 111–13). As these kites moved upward, they too drew the eye farther into the sky, and although large on the ground, they soon hovered far away, becoming tiny marks on the vastness of an incredible blue canvas. Where this koan was taking me would be the rest of my life.

The time spent in Japan passed too quickly. I made many kites there, and by the time my stay neared its close I had become reasonably skillful with bamboo and paper. My kites were exhibited in a one-man show in Tokyo's most prestigious modern-art gallery, the Minami.

After returning to the United States I received a letter from Japan enumerating all that had happened since my departure. My friend concluded, "Time flies!" It does indeed, but as I remarked earlier, it also seems that time frequently stops when kites are flying. There are, of course, other activities that produce the same or a similar feeling of well-being. Children discover them without being told; adults have to be reminded. I often think it would be nice if children started out playing golf and going fishing and ended up as adults flying kites.

88. A striking kite with a design of a flying crane. From Hamamatsu, Shizuoka Prefecture.

89. The pulley men are the team's strongest members, since they are the ones who actually hold back the kite while it flies. Notice the gloves used as protection against rope burns. Hamamatsu, Shizuoka Prefecture.

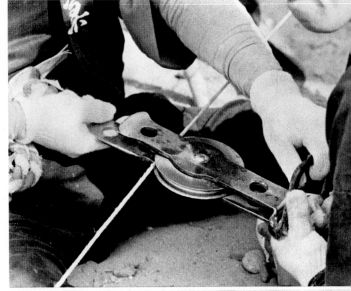

90. Up goes a beautiful kite at the Hamamatsu festival held each April on the Nakatajima grounds. Hamamatsu, Shizuoka Prefecture.

91. Flyers readying a kite for fighting. The vertical and horizontal bones of the kite crisscross, making it resemble shoji, Japanese sliding doors. Hamamatsu, Shizuoka Prefecture.

92. (opposite) Hauling the flying line during the kite fighting at the Hamamatsu festival. Hamamatsu, Shizuoka Prefecture.

93. Shingo Modegi—restaurateur, world traveler, and kite addict—with several kites from his extensive collection. Tokyo.

94. (right) The Nagasaki kite maker Kohei Morimoto in his workshop. Nagasaki. See Plates 54–56 for Morimoto kites.

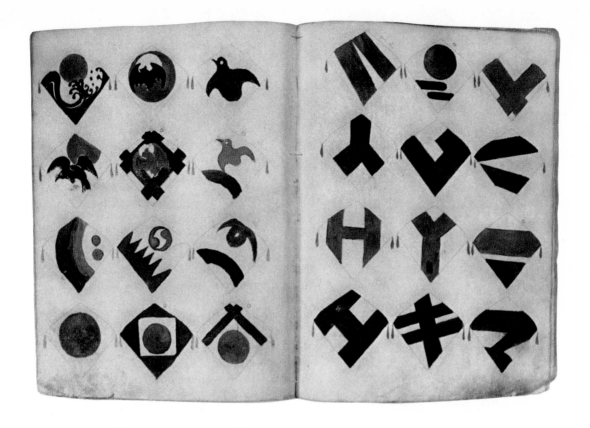

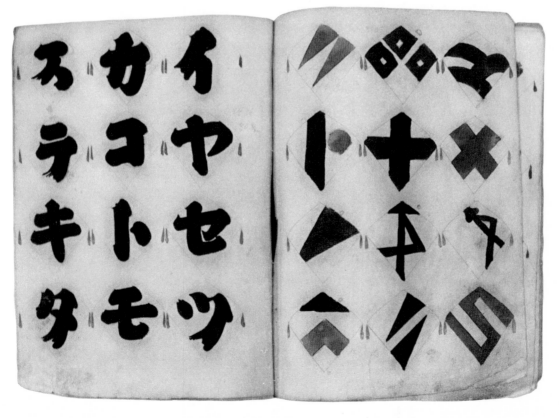

95–96. Pages from Nagasaki kite maker Shigeyoshi Morimoto's kite pattern book, dated 1931.

97–100. The giant Hoshubana Showa o-dako is first pushed up on edge and temporarily tied to a scaffold so that 200 separate bridle lines can be easily attached to it. This is followed by the liftoff. The great size of the kite makes some spectators wonder if it will really leave the ground. It weighs nearly a ton and is 48 by 36 feet. Hoshubana, Saitama Prefecture. Courtesy of Hoshubana O-dako Association.

101. The flying team, kite association members, and a Shinto priest (extreme left) pose for a formal photograph before the annual flying of the Hoshubana Showa o-dako. Hoshubana, Saitama Prefecture. Courtesy of Hoshubana O-dako Association.

102. A bamboo stalk.

105. Removing impurities from the pulp. Like many paper-making tasks, this cold, arduous one is performed in winter. Courtesy of David Hughes.

103–4. The white inner bark of the *kozo* branch, a type of mulberry, is the basic material for handmade Japanese paper. Here it is being washed in a clear, cold mountain stream and dried for three or four days to rid it of its gummy residue. Courtesy of Mamoru Iwasaki.

106. A mixture of paper-making ingredients is placed on a screen, and a rocking motion allows it to settle evenly.

107. The final step of paper making: drying damp sheets of paper on smooth boards in the afternoon sun. Courtesy of David Hughes.

108–9. Tsutomu Hiroi and his raincoat kite on a Tokyo roof.

110. (opposite left) Tsutomu Hiroi's caterpillar kite in flight.

111–12. (opposite, center and right) These two kite drawings, done in colored pencil on graph paper in 1970, are titled "Red Line in the Sky" and "Roll-up Flying Red Line." Both are in the collection of New York's Museum of Modern Art.

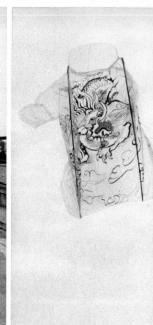

113. On Miho Beach, Shizuoka Prefecture, where I flew kites like the one I'm carrying here. Courtesy of Randy Phillips.

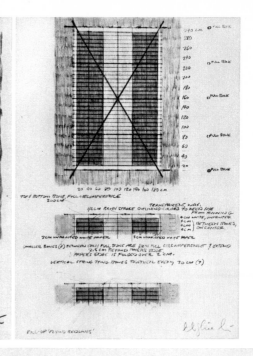

title: red line in the sky

ROLL-UP 'FLYING REDLINES'

114. In a print by Hokusai, the warrior Minamoto no Tametomo is shown helping his son escape from their isle of exile by lashing him to a kite to be flown to the mainland. Courtesy of Heibonsha.

115. *The Mitsui Store in the Suruga District*, by Hokusai. With snow-capped Fuji in the distance, Hokusai suggests the New Year season by including kites traditionally flown at that time. Courtesy of Shibundo.

116. Planing thin bones that have been split from a large bamboo stalk.

117. Replacing paper in a kite damaged in flight.

118. Painting a kite. To keep the dye from running in the absorbent paper, outlines have been painted in paraffin.

119. A 15-foot roll-up kite in preparation. The paper has been glued to the framework and is being held in place by the stones and pieces of bamboo.

120–26. A variety of string, spools, and reels used in kite flying.

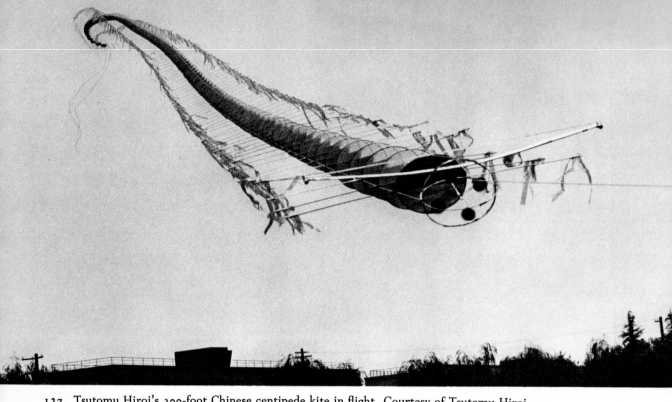

127. Tsutomu Hiroi's 300-foot Chinese centipede kite in flight. Courtesy of Tsutomu Hiroi.

129–30. Two tiny kites, a Suruga Yoshitsune and a Tsugaru, about 3 by 5 inches each.

128. A tiny Edo kite, about 2 1/2 by 4 inches. Courtesy of Tsutomu Hiroi.

13

ORIENTAL KITES:
A BRIEF HISTORY

THE KITE'S BEGINNINGS

MUCH OF THE HISTORY of the past two to three hundred years of Japanese kites and kite festivals follows regional lines of development. The ancient history of the kite as it is known in Japan, however, begins in China and Korea.

The first stories tell of a wooden kite in the form of a dove invented in China by a contemporary of Confucius (551–479 B.C.). Some historians attribute this wooden bird—which may or may not have been a kite—to Lord Rohan (or Lu Pan in Chinese), who was a famous craftsman, mechanic, and architect of China. Lord Rohan plays a minor but prestigious role in the charming folk fairy tale written in the eighteenth century by Roku-jiuyen and since translated as *The Magical Carpenter of Japan*. In the story, Lord Rohan comes from Paradise on a purple cloud to escort the magical carpenter back to help in the completion of the splendid Palace of the Moon. The magical carpenter, "full of the spirit of his craft, got beyond mere saw and chisel work, and fashioned the most wonderful creatures of sky and land: birds out of ends of wood and horses out of slabs of timber; in fact he was the marvel of his time."

The carpenter of the fairy tale resembles Lord Rohan, who was a real person, while stories about Lord Rohan sound suspiciously like fairy tales. There are many variations, for example, on the story of his wonderful wooden bird kite. Some relate that the wooden bird flew up and away into the sky, never to return. In another tale, told in a more realistic and Confucianist mode, it is reported that the bird kite had only limited success—that is, Rohan profited from the knowledge gained by his failure. Perhaps we hear the ring of truth in such prosaic storytelling. The question that naturally arises of whether the wooden dove was a mechanical bird or a kite on a line is virtually unresolvable. Popular acceptance of the device as a kite, however, may be a reflection of the difficulty we would be facing if we credited Rohan with the invention of the airplane.

Given the fact that the ancient Chinese were diligent historians, we might expect that this work by a well-known figure would be carefully documented. Unfortunately, however, most of the volumes of history written around this period were destroyed. They were burned by Shih Huang Ti, or the "First Emperor," of the Ch'in dynasty (255–207 B.C.) in an attempt to ensure that only his history, the history of Ch'in, would remain.

It is in the period immediately preceding Shih Huang Ti's reign that kites probably made their first appearance. The earliest written attribution for the invention of the kite does not occur, however, until the Liu Sung, or Former Sung, period (A.D. 420–79). In a book called *Shih Wu Chi Yuan* it is noted that in 200 B.C. Han Hsin, a famous statesman, adviser, and general to the first emperor of the Han dynasty (206 B.C.–A.D. 7), invented the kite for the purpose of measuring the length of a tunnel needed to broach the walls of an enemy palace. This is the most widely accepted version of the kite's invention. There are, however, several elaborations on this story.

The favorite version of children calls attention to Han Hsin's unusually diminutive size, which was close to the stature of a child. In this tale, Han Hsin had himself tied to a large kite during a campaign against enemy armies and then was flown over the enemy camp at night. From this frightening object passing over their heads in the darkening sky, the soldiers below heard a command telling them to return to their families. They were needed at home, the voice warned, and would die if they remained. Many of them fled, and the next day Han Hsin and his soldiers easily routed the few remaining frightened and demoralized enemy. Of the many kite shapes favored by children that have evolved in China, one is that of a man with wings. On it, perhaps in reference to Han Hsin's small size and in homage to his great intellect, sometimes appears the legend, "Strength of mind is greater than strength of body."

The children's version may be an amalgamation involving another general, this one still loyal to the Ch'in court, who attempted to unseat the Han emperor Liu Pang. This unfortunate general, when surrounded by the superior strength of the Han army, devised the scheme of attaching tautly bowed strings to his kite. The kite was flown into the wind at night over the Han camp, and its bowed strings shrieked and howled in a most terrifying manner, causing the Han forces to retreat in terror. "Hummers" modeled on this principle are still used in China and Japan. (The Chinese word for kite interestingly enough is *feng cheng*, or "wind harp," as the Chinese kite is commonly flown with hummers or reed pipes.) The name "hummer" is a misnomer; the unearthly shrieks and wails produced by this device still frighten poor souls out of their wits. As a testament to their unpleasantness—which only increases the pleasure of the flyers—hummers have frequently been outlawed by Japanese municipalities. As late as World War II, they were banned because their screaming sound was too easily mistaken for that of falling bombs.

In Korea, in the middle of the fourteenth century, a famous general was sent to Cheju Island off the southern coast to quell a farmers' rebellion. "When his fleet sailed close to the island, near the enemy castle of Ziza-song, he found that the coast was so steep and rough that there was no place where his soldiers could land. So he conceived the idea of launching fire-carrying kites from the ship over the enemy castle," writes Sang-su Choe in *The Survey of Korean Kites*. Another version of this story suggests that he flew his men on big kites directly from the ship over the castle walls.

The most reliable compilation of ancient Korean history is one of Korea's earliest books *Samguk Sagi,* or *History of the Three Kingdoms,* written in A.D. 1145. The book documents an event that took place in the seventh century. Its authenticity is reasonably certain: "In the first year of Queen Zindong, the 28th ruler of the Silla dynasty, there was a revolt by Bi-dam and Yom-zong. Gim Yu-Sin [A.D. 596–637], a famous general, undertook a mission to subdue the rebels. During this military operation, one evening it happened that a large star suddenly appeared and fell toward the earth near the castle named Wol-song. It was generally believed in those days that a falling star was a bad omen, especially during wartime. It meant that terrible bloodshed and disaster would come. So the people and soldiers began to feel uneasy. To make the situation worse, rumors went around that where the star had fallen terrible bloodshed would ensue and their queen would be defeated. This made the people and soldiers extremely nervous and uneasy. It seemed to be very difficult to control the agitated public. General Gim Yu-Sin thought that he had to find some means of carrying a fireball high up in the sky, and let it disappear. A kite could do this. One evening a fireball going up into the sky was seen by the people who believed that the fallen star had gone back to heaven. With the soldiers' morale boosted, General Gim Yu-Sin was able to control the public and destroy the rebels."

Firecrackers hanging from the tails of Chinese kites are commonplace even today. Long-burning fuses or punk cause them to explode at erratic intervals long after they have left the ground. I have never heard of anyone attaching firecrackers to kites in Japan, although I don't doubt that it has been done, for the Japanese love fireworks.

There are innumerable instances in the Far East of kites being used for military purposes. They were frequently employed as signals. For example, in the first century A.D., a Liang-dynasty emperor, while under siege in his palace, sent kites flying up over the battlements in a prearranged signal for help. As his message was relayed across the countryside, more kites appeared in the fields nearby. Soon a rural army appeared and dispelled the attackers. Such signal kites, with noisy hummers or reed pipes attached, would not be overlooked by people bent at their work in the fields. Kites had other martial uses. Secret messages were commonly sent by them, and they carried food and supplies to the defenders of besieged castles. Large kites capable of carrying a man were flown over castle walls as a means of escape for those trapped by enemy forces. They also provided lofty platforms from which enemy activities could be observed. One wonders at the success of such ventures. In spite of the obvious dangers, all of them were possible—with the help of luck and divine winds.

THE CULTURE OF CHINA spread to Japan in two waves from two of China's richest dynasties. The first wave, which arrived around 200 B.C., brought rice farming, bronze, and iron to Japan, which was still in its stone age. At that time the Han dynasty was to the East what Rome was to the West. The second wave occurred around A.D. 500. During this period, that of the T'ang dynasty (618–907), China was the richest, strongest, and most advanced country in the world, East or West. Japan eagerly accepted T'ang culture and for two centuries, things Chinese were eagerly sought after: principles of government, civil law, literature, arts, and Buddhism.

Buddhism was a missionary religion that had moved from India into China via the Silk Road. Now it moved farther east to Korea, and through Korea into Japan. Traveling with Buddhism, and in its service, were Chinese and Korean artists: bronze casters, sculptors, lacquerers, metal workers, carpenters, calligraphers, painters . . . and, most likely, kite makers.

When they arrived, Japan was predominantly an agricultural community. Wind, sun, rain, and the cycle of the seasons were at the heart of its institutions. The emergence of a court (the ancestors of the present imperial family), the introduction of Buddhism, and the centralization of government in Nara fostered the growth of the arts. The immigrant artists who came to Nara needed many assistants to help them with their work. These assistants were drawn from among the young men of Japan's lower classes, generally sons of poor farmers who might otherwise have remained victims of the harsh rural life. Some of the new assistants were no doubt also attracted to the bustle of activity around Nara. It was not only Japan's first capital, but its first actual city as well. What the young men brought with them were the sensitivities and skills of farmers so useful to an artist: familiarity with tools, intimacy with nature, and that feeling for life itself that has to be implied in inanimate objects of art. Working side by side with the immigrant masters, these eager apprentices quickly showed an aptitude for their new work. They were, in fact, the precursors of the main streams of Japan's art.

We may theorize that kites came to Japan during the Nara period (649–794). From the sixth through the eighth century, many Japanese intent on studying Buddhism closer to its roots traveled to China, while continental Buddhists came to Japan. Somewhere along the way a kite was brought to Japan. The kite seems a humble enough object that it need not have been seriously related to Buddhism or to the early Nara craftsmen. But because Buddhist priests at a much later date used kites for religious purposes, it is possible that the kite was associated with the early Buddhist missionary work. The early use of kites in China and Korea for military purposes demonstrates that kites were not taken lightly during this period of history. No doubt one who knew the secrets of kite making was held in high regard and had disciples and apprentices as did the other artists of the period. But this is all guesswork. The only fact we are left with in the end is that there is no known documentation of the kite's introduction to Japan. As the *Encyclopaedia Britannica* blithely concludes after having attributed the kite's invention to the West, "but they have been in use among Asian peoples from time immemorial."

The first book in Japan to record the word "kite" was the dictionary *Wamyo Ruiju Sho,* compiled by Minamoto Shitago in A.D. 981. Kites were then called *kami tobi,* or paper hawks. This suggests that they were shaped like birds. Chinese kites of this period are most generally recorded as being rectangular, although there may have been earlier bird kites, as the "wooden dove" story suggests. Bird, insect, human, and dragon kite forms became quite common in China and Japan. Korean kites, on the other hand, modeled on the early rectangular Chinese kites, remained exclusively rectangular (with a large hole cut out of the center to aid stability).

There is a variety of regional words for kite in Japan today. One of these, *tako* (and its variant form *dako*) may be translated as either "kite" or "octopus." The written characters for kite and octopus are different, but when the words are spoken they are indistinguishable, except from their context. The choice of a spoken word for kite that was already being used for octopus is an instance of a play on words that refers to one of the early kite shapes based on the form of the octopus (Plate 69). The large body is the kite proper, and its eight tentacles are the paper tails that writhe realistically in a breeze. *Ika* ("squid") is an alternative term for kite, as is *ika nobori* ("squid banner"). In Nagasaki an early word for kite was *ago,* from *ago-bata,* or flying fish. The kite form was that of a fish. Another term used in Nagasaki was *komori-bata,* or flying bat. *Bata,* from *batabata,* may be more specifically translated as "flapping or fluttering wings." The present word for kite in Nagasaki, *hata,* translates as "flag" or "banner." Tako, however, is by far the most commonly used designation surviving today throughout Japan. Tako is a Tokyo dialect word. It has been suggested that it may be a play on the word "Tokyo," a reference to the kite's close identification with Tokyo in the eighteenth century, when kites streamed out of the capital city to delight the rest of the country.

FESTIVAL AND CELEBRATION KITES

KITES HAVE NEVER stood alone in Japan, but have always been associated with festivals, holidays, and other special occasions for celebration.

Before the arrival of Buddhism in the sixth century, the chief feature of the native Japanese religion was worship of the mysterious powers that were believed to rule nature. On appropriate occasions the people offered rites to the gods of nature, praying for benevolent weather and plentiful crops. With the passing of time, it became the custom to observe a festival in the spring and autumn. The formal religion of Shinto evolved out of rites at such festivals. With the introduction of Buddhism, Shinto did not disappear; instead the two became complementary religions. Once again hypothesizing, it seems likely that Buddhist priests from China and Korea first introduced their countries' kites into Japan's religious festivals. Just who introduced them is open to speculation, but as late as the end of the seventeenth century kites were still closely associated with religious festivals. From the atmosphere and circumstances of the Nara period, which was intensely religious, we may deduce that Japan's kites were most likely associated with religion first, and only later with secular activities.

By the beginning of the eighteenth century, kite history is more certain. Kites then were flown as invocations for a rich harvest. Buddhist priests also held that the kite's flight could predict the success or failure of a forthcoming crop, a kind of divination. With the coming of autumn, festival kites were flown as thanksgiving offerings for a plentiful harvest. In some areas it was the custom to tie stalks of rice to the kite as a kind of symbolic offering of thanks. Priests customarily gave their blessing to all such kites. In some religions, kites could be purchased at temples and shrines as charms against sickness and misfortune. Whether or not they were efficacious, such charms often degenerated into kites too small and too heavy to fly. Kites may also have been flown as a part of other religious services, and it will be remembered from the chapter on the giant Hoshubana kites that Buddhist priests helped spread knowledge of the use of kites for predicting weather.

Other kites not nominally connected with religion but frequently given to worshipers by Shinto and Buddhist priests were congratulatory kites. These kites were given to the parents of firstborn sons. Such kites were also given by the child's grandparents and by friends or town officials, depending on the status of the family. These kites bore appropriate messages or paintings of folk heroes or of the gods who would protect and guide a newborn son toward a good and prosperous adulthood. Kintaro, Golden Boy, was one of the favored pictures for these congratulatory kites. Kintaro, also called Kintoki, was abandoned in a mountain forest by a family so poor that they could not raise him. He was adopted by bears and grew up to be one of Japan's strongest and most valiant men. On kites, Kintaro's round red face is often paired with a picture of a carp, another symbol of strength and bravery because it must swim upstream to propagate its species (Plates 45, 72, 83).

Japan's New Year kites have been flown from some unrecorded moment in the past until the present as symbolic offerings of thanks for the benevolence of the gods in the past year and hope for a good new year (Plate 115). For some kite flyers the past year may have brought a firstborn son. And others may have flown a kite out of gratitude for nothing more than still being alive. On New Year kites appear Kintaro; the crane and tortoise (the former is said to live a hundred years; the latter, a thousand); Fukusuke, a large-headed dwarf; Daruma, the Buddhist sage whose legs withered away in nine years of meditation; countless brave warriors of history and mythology; and menacing, fierce *oni* demons or ogres.

In Korea, New Year kites are flown for the first fifteen days of the first moon. Shortly after that time, a kite is flown with the message, "Bad luck away, good luck stay." This kite is flown out to the end of its string, and then both kite and string are released. The freed kite takes with it all the bad luck its owner might have been destined to endure during the forthcoming year. Such a kite will not be picked up if found, for fear of acquiring misfortune. Bad luck is left to disintegrate with the kite through the winter winds and snows. The same tradition prevailed from the first to the ninth of September in China. Anyone finding a fallen kite after the ninth was required by custom to burn it.

Although festival and religious kite lore in Japan was not well documented until the beginning of the eighteenth century, when kites are mentioned frequently, we may guess that ceremonial usage of them began much earlier, perhaps as early as the sixth century. Within the past two to three hundred years what has emerged is a transition from the deeply religious to the quasi-religious, with religion's patronage or sponsorship being replaced by the secular pleasure of kite flying.

Japan's religions have always had close ties to nature, the seasons, and growth cycles. Speaking broadly, they have been characterized by benevolence and pleasure rather than wrath and penance. When kites were employed in religious ceremonies, they functioned as pleasurable intermediaries between the sacred and the profane. In recent times, what has remained of the sacred are scraps of ceremony and token vestiges of past observances. Although the kite may still appear on a festival or religious holiday, a Japanese today, unless he is very old, does not accept the direction a kite falls out of the sky as a prophecy of the year's rice crop. And the Japanese child receives the good wishes of a New Year kite much as a Westerner accepts a birthday or Christmas present.

Nevertheless, the kite still stands as an intermediary between the religious and secular spheres, only now its links are much closer to the latter. This shift mirrors the general tendency among postwar Japanese in their daily life to place far more emphasis on secular affairs than on those of a religious nature. It should be noted, however, that distinctions between these two kinds of activity are seldom so marked in Japan as they are in the West; and so there is much overlapping of the two. In any case, it appears that something of the original religious purpose of the kite as viewed by the early priests has remained through the centuries to the present day—that of providing wholesome pleasure.

FIGHTING KITES

THE JAPANESE FESTIVALS incorporating congratulatory kites and harvest thanksgiving evolved into yet another kind of activity, that of kite fighting. Although kite fighting appears to have been well established in China and Korea by the time kites entered Japan, it does not seem that this custom was immediately taken up by the Japanese. Kite fighting, because it can bring about loss of face, in Japan may have required an unintentional match to get started. Or perhaps an extremely disgruntled flyer was goaded into crossing strings with a neighbor's kite, unceremoniously pulling it down out of the sky. Its origins aside, kite fighting never gained widespread popularity in Japan, but where it did catch on, the enthusiasm of the participants knew no bounds. As a release from the formality of Japanese society and the harsh conditions of rural life, it provided a much-needed outlet.

Kite fighting followed basically the same combative pattern in Japan, India, China, and Korea: generally small, highly maneuverable kites were attached to strings partly coated with powdered glass (when it was available), sharp sand, or ground pottery, and sometimes scythelike knife blades. A kite fighter tried to bring another kite down out of the sky by skillful maneuvering. By crossing the opponent's kite line with his own and moving it back and forth, he could wear away or cut the other kite's flying line. At this point the loser's kite floated away free, while the victor proclaimed his invincibility and challenged all bystanders. In Japan, Nagasaki flyers are the most notable proponents of this type of fighting. Kite fighting there, as we saw earlier, dates from the early seventeenth century.

Kite battles take place any time during the flying season in India, China, Korea, and Japan. In Japan, the informality and small kites that characterize kite flying in the other three countries seem to have evolved into well-organized festival fighting with the participants flying increasingly larger kites. Nagasaki is the only district I know of where one might still consider a kite flying alone in the sky as an invitation for another to attack it. Local customs, fun, or devilishness, however, could prevail to keep informal kite fighting alive though undocumented in many other areas.

Although kites are traditionally associated with boys, young girls today may also fly kites. At big kite festivals, girls may also help with the flying. This happens in Shirone, where informality is the rule, but not in Hamamatsu, where kite flying is highly organized as a kind of male gymnastics.

In Japan, where large areas of open space are virtually nonexistent, finding a place for informal kite flying can be a challenge. At the New Year, if the rice paddies are not planted with another crop, the hard ground is suitable for a kite-flying field. In the summer, however, either rice is maturing or the rice bed is still muddy. In either case if a kite flyer runs along the high, narrow paths of the paddy dikes, he faces the unpleasant prospect of a fall into mud or rough rice stubble. As the most popular alternative, Japan's wide riverbeds generally contain dry areas during most of the year. These riverbeds are the most favored locations for kite flying, particularly for city dwellers. For people fortunate enough to live beside the sea or ocean, the sandy beaches and ocean breezes are ideal for kite flying.

GIANT KITES

THERE IS A FASCINATION with the very small and the very large in the East. In Japan, an artist is said to have been greatly admired for having carved sixty-six monkeys from a single peach pit. In India one may still buy a tiny shell filled with one hundred ivory elephants so tiny that they must be identified with the aid of a magnifying glass. Chinese miniatures are well known. The great woodblock artist Hokusai (1760–1849) once painted a portrait of Daruma sixty feet high, and also drew two sparrows on a single grain of rice. Having proved his skill in the two extremes of scale, his ordinary-sized works could hardly be questioned. In Japan, every kite maker offers tiny replicas—made to fly—of his regular-size kites. And those I visited always mentioned that they had at one time or another been commissioned to make giant kites.

Giant kites have never failed to capture the imagination of the Japanese. In the late seventeenth century large kites were employed on one occasion for lifting tiles to the roof of a great temple. More romantically, and perhaps taking his inspiration from the practical tile-lifting kite, the daring robber Kakinoki Kinsuke (also known as Kakinomura Kinsuke) in

1712 had himself tied to a kite and flown to the roof of Nagoya Castle in an attempt to steal the golden dolphins (valued at about half a million dollars) at either end of the ridgepole course. Legend says that he was successful in pulling off some of the dolphins' golden scales; history, however, records that he and his family were boiled in oil for his numerous crimes.

An earlier legend of someone riding a giant kite says that in the twelfth century Minamoto no Tametomo (a hero of the famous Genji clan) and his son were exiled from the capital, then in Kyoto, to Hachijo, the outermost of the seven Izu Islands. Tametomo is supposed to have attempted to return his son to the mainland via a big kite (Plate 114). There is a tiny body of land within 4 miles of Hachijo, the next nearest island is 50 miles away, and the mainland itself is 108 miles distant. I mention these distances not in skepticism, but in an attempt to consider seriously the plausibility of an adventure now clouded in legend. I heard of Tametomo and his son often from a number of sources, but no one ever mentioned the feat as a real possibility. From my point of view, flight to the nearest island would have been extremely difficult—but not impossible. The people who live on Hachijo are still aroused by the legend, for big kites appear there periodically and the Hachijo kite traditionally carries a picture of Tametomo and his quiver of arrows.

There are similar stories involving unfortunate men, exiled prisoners who were forced to work in the gold and silver mines of Sado Island in the Japan Sea. In this case man-carrying kites would have required a flying line 15 miles long to reach the mainland. Again, difficult but perhaps not impossible.

A man-carrying kite would have to be big, but there have been some far larger than is necessary for the task. At least one was large enough to carry a man, together with his wife and child, and perhaps even a small grandmother. Though it in fact did not take on passengers, the largest kite in the world until its demise in 1914 was known as the *wanwan* (Plate 74), which was made and flown in the city of Naruto in Shikoku.

This kite was the apotheosis of Japan's ability to enlarge things normally associated with a modest scale to a size almost beyond comprehension. Reports of the actual size of giant, out-of-the-ordinary objects in Japan tend to be quite contradictory. This is not surprising, for one is hard pressed for accuracy or a point of reference when confronted with such unbelievable size. The following figures, with attendant qualifications, are, I believe, reliable: The wanwan kite, made of bamboo and paper, came in a variety of sizes from small to giant. The largest version was sixty-three feet in diameter; its shape was round but slightly flattened on the horizontal. This kite, together with its bridle and tail, weighed 8,800 pounds. Depending on the wind, 150 to 200 men were required to fly it. The great kite was flown annually in a summer festival from the middle of the nineteenth century until 1914. Eyewitnesses to the wanwan festivals over the years variously reported that the kite was sixty to sixty-five feet in diameter and weighed from as little as 1,700 pounds to as much as 5,500 pounds. In fact, the size of the giant wanwan varied from year to year. Also, large numbers of kites of different sizes were flown from day to day in the same festival period. The apparent discrepancies in weight can be accounted for by the varying sizes as well as by the inclusion or exclusion in the total of the weight of the bridle and flying line. Thirty-five to one hundred separate bridle lines, depending on the kite's size, would have been required. These lines add considerably to a kite's weight, and as a kite is actually lifting this weight, it is not unreasonable to count the bridles and flying line in the total weight of a kite. The wanwan required a huge tail to help stabilize its flight; the largest wanwan required one five hundred feet long that was made from lengths of heavy ship rope.

Strong sea winds carried the huge kite aloft. Retrieving it was even more difficult than sending it skyward. The winch that let out the heavy flying line was held securely by virtue of being buried deep in the ground. Winch-reeling it in, however, was often impossible. An alternative was to walk it in; that is, using a technique whereby the flyers walk down the line toward the kite, in this way shortening the flying line and causing the kite to come down. Not infrequently, the wind was too strong for the kite to be safely retrieved even with the combined strength of two hundred men. In such cases it had to be left flying until the wind died, allowing it to fall back to earth of its own accord.

There are still a few professional kite makers, among them Mampei Tadokoro of Naruto, who keep the secrets of the giant wanwan shape. Given the fact that there are still those who know how to make the giant kite, it is difficult to imagine that it will not one day fly again. Such traditions resist dying out in Japan, reviving at the last possible moment to begin again with renewed fervor.

Of the remaining giant kites being flown today in Japan, in the Shirone and Hoshubana festivals, the Hoshubana o-dako forty-eight feet high by thirty-six feet wide is the largest. The old wanwan, by way of comparison, would have been roughly one-and-a-half times the size of the Hoshubana o-dako.

THE RECENT PAST

FOR SOME INEXPLICABLE REASON, around the middle of the eighteenth century kites became the rage in Tokyo. The enthusiasm for them grew and quickly spread across Japan. It is difficult for us to visualize now, but beginning in January and continuing through May, Japan's skies were virtually never empty of kites. An encyclopedia of 1911 records that merchants could often be seen flying kites from the doorways of their shops while waiting for customers. The mania gradually tapered off, but some of its life still remained into the first decades of the twentieth century.

In the beginning everyone, it seemed, both children and adults, flew kites. Kite makers were unable to keep up with the demand. During this period at least, the kite maker was a financially successful member of the community. As a consequence, men from less successful occupations were attracted to kite making, as it offered the hope of a new life. Many others worked part time to help the professional kite maker fill his orders and to supplement their own meager incomes. (Japan's kite mania was not some curious Eastern malady; it was also felt in Europe. In France riots broke out between flyers, and in 1736 kite flying in public places was outlawed there.)

The government was concerned about this new rage, for it appeared to cause people to forget their work. Men in the fields, upon seeing kites flying from a nearby field, could not, it seems, resist the impulse to raise their own kites into the sky. Then, overtaken by the euphoria that still characterizes kite flying today, work in the fields was forgotten. The countless edicts issued in a vain effort to curtail kite flying, even outlawing it entirely on many occasions, proved difficult to enforce and were largely ignored.

The popularity of the kite in Japan had sped from Edo down the Tokaido Road and out into the surrounding countryside. At about the same time, the inexpensive, colorful ukiyo-e prints came into vogue. These too spread by the same route into the country, and there both art forms were popular as inexpensive gifts. As with kites, the government tried to control this new diversion by such measures as placing a ban on the use of bright colors. Ukiyo-e artists were closely watched by the authorities and an artist occasionally went to jail when one of his pictures appeared to cast aspersion on the samurai class.

The suitability of ukiyo-e-style drawing and colors to his own product quickly became apparent to the kite maker. Often he was asked to paint in this fashion on his kites. A combination of the demand for ukiyo-e and, possibly, the kite maker's own eye for the artfulness of the prints helped them to become a standard by which he could judge his own work. Not all kite makers followed this trend, but many did, accepting as a part of their training the study of ukiyo-e drawing and coloring as well as the subjects of ukiyo-e, particularly those of the Kabuki theater, which the commoner enjoyed and wanted depicted on his kites. It was during the Edo period that the kite reached its peak in popularity. The adoption of ukiyo-e-style drawing generally marked the end of the kite's evolution, and the designs that became more or less fixed then are still used in kite making.

In 1868 the shogun's government collapsed. The Tokugawa family had kept the peace in Japan for over two centuries, but their time was up. For the first time in more than six hundred years, the government was run by civilians, although most of them came from the now-defunct warrior class. And for the first time in more than two hundred years, Japan was open to foreign intercourse.

The revitalized nation then began an extraordinary process of modernization and westernization in which countless traditional practices were altered or completely done away with. Commoners, who had not been allowed to have surnames, now were given the rights to be known by a full name. This meant that for the first time all artists were allowed to sign their work, whereas anonymity had been the rule in many arts. Works continued to be produced anonymously by some artists for a time but eventually the practice of signing one's work became the rule rather than the exception. The kite maker, however, appears to have remained satisfied with anonymity. He continued to sign his kites Yokosuka-dako, Suruga Tako Hachi, Edo-dako, Shirone rokkaku, or Nagasaki hata, names that identified the maker only by his location. Today there are about 130 kite makers spread throughout Japan, still relatively anonymous.

All futures are uncertain, the Japanese kite's perhaps more so than most. Some observers believe kite making in Japan is a dying art. They cite the fact that many of the present kite makers are very old and have no successors, and they recall the Tokyo statistics: one hundred kite makers, then thirty-five, now one, soon none. However bad the situation seems, there are young and middle-aged men (and one woman) who are still dedicated to the traditions of the professional kite maker. And one may be certain that the major kite festivals are alive and healthy. It is difficult to imagine them disappearing in the near or even distant future. The Japanese have demonstrated in countless ways an enviable capacity for modernizing without letting go of the past, for reaching back to the rich storehouse of the nation's past and rediscovering neglected or all but forgotten beauty.

14

MAKE YOUR OWN KITE
AND FLY IT

MAKE A JAPANESE KITE?

THIS CHAPTER PROVIDES INFORMATION of a deliberately general nature about the making of several kinds of Japanese kites, with particular emphasis on the Suruga and Nagasaki kites. It is not my intention in this chapter to teach the reader how to make a Japanese kite; instead, I hope that from the examples I will give here the reader may move closer to making a kite of his own design.

When I first arrived in Japan I was eager to learn as much as possible about kites in as short a time as possible. I had been forewarned, however, that in Japan, where traditional skills have been faithfully acquired and passed down through generations, I would be poorly received if I did not adjust my pace to that of the tradition-minded kite makers. To prepare for my first meeting with one, I tried gathering some preliminary information about Japanese kites. To this end I asked each new acquaintance, however casual, questions about kite making. What kind of paste was used? What were the brilliant colors made from? What was the best kind of paper? Where could I find the right kind of bamboo? I pestered people for information about anything that might help me to begin making kites as soon as possible. The answers were not always immediately forthcoming; not every Japanese, I quickly learned, was schooled in the details of kite making. But answers did come back to me, often a few days or a week after they were asked. Everyone, it seemed, was eager to help as much as they could. Then I met my first Japanese kite maker, Tatsu-saburo Kato.

I found the shop of this master kite maker within weeks of my arrival at my new home in Shizuoka. Kato met my inquiries about the Suruga kite and kite making in general with barely disguised ill-humor. He had worked diligently to learn the craft of kite making since he was a youth of sixteen. He was now seventy-three, and it did not appear that he was willing to share almost sixty years of hard-earned knowledge with a young American amateur. It was a disturbing setback, the more so because it was unexpected.

Then, quite by accident, I found out the reason for Kato's brusqueness at our initial meetings. What had happened was that everyone I queried with my kite-making problems, eager to help but unable to, had immediately hurried to Kato's shop to learn the answers to my questions! My acquaintances knew as little of kite making as I did, for this was the work of a professional. Kato was understandably annoyed and reluctant to spend time with the brash foreigner whose persistent questioning had so often caused the relative quiet of the kite maker's life to be disturbed. What might such a man do in person! I sympathized with his distress and wrote him a letter, asking to be excused for the disturbance I had in-advertently caused, and explained that I was like a baby about kites in Japan and very fond of them. I apologized and said that I hoped he would forgive me.

As far as Kato was concerned, I assumed a low profile—very low. I proceeded instead to learn about kite making through my own experiments. The information I requested from my acquaintances, meager in the beginning, began to multiply as time passed. My bamboo supplier offered to make inquiries about specific problems I had in the course of my ex-periments. With each of my worried requests that he not ask Kato anything, he assured me that his expert lived in another district and was, in fact, a fisherman who had given up kite making long ago as a young man.

During the time I lived in Japan, I was frequently interviewed for Japanese newspapers and magazines. The articles dealt primarily with my sculpture, but kites were often men-tioned when invariably the reporters found me at home surrounded by Japanese kites, down on my hands and knees pasting together sheets of paper for my own kites. They generally reported that I greatly respected master kite maker Kato. I hoped he saw the articles.

Finally I was nearly ready to leave Japan, and I had yet to talk at length with Kato. I decided to try one last time to see him. A friend delivered by hand my very formal request for a meeting. She soon sent me a note describing their meeting: "He looked as stubborn as usual, but I found him to be in fairly good humor. After he had run his eyes through your letter, he said roughly 'After the twentieth of this month I will not be at home. If he's coming it must be before the twentieth!'"

Our meeting turned out to be a friendly one. The things he told me were interesting; that he held back about certain matters was also of interest. Through his pride I grasped an attitude that I would like to pass along here. Simply stated, it is this: Suruga-dako must not be diluted by imitation or export. Kato himself, unlike many Japanese kite makers attempting to survive in a time when kite interest has diminished, has firmly refused to make his kites for export. Some do find their way out of Japan, but only a small number. Suruga-dako is essentially a kite that has lived and will die, if it must, in the Suruga Bay area. If one cares to keep such a kite alive himself, he must go to Shizuoka, apprentice himself to this master kite maker and spend the rest of his life there learning about and making the Suruga kite. Less than this is thievery.

Kato said none of this directly, but it is clear to me that this is not an exaggeration of his feelings. Around Shizuoka now, gross imitations of the Suruga-dako fly in the sky, poorly drawn faces printed by machine in cheap colors on paper that quickly discolors. Such kites sell for less than those made patiently and beautifully by Kato's hands. Though their owners are probably unaware of it, the pleasure these poor copies give is considerably less than would be derived from Kato's originals. And they are the poorer for it. The imitations are uncommonly ugly in my eyes, for I know that they serve to make Kato poorer as he nears the end of his life.

General Characteristics of the Japanese Kite

THIS SECTION ATTEMPTS to add generally technical information, information gained primarily from Japanese sources, to that which might be found in books specifically written as kite-making manuals or guides. For the reader who is not interested in technical information, I have attempted to include my attitude toward kite making and something of the spirit of kite making.

Most of the Japanese kites being made today are based on three- or four-hundred-year-old models. These models are flat or bow-faced kites. The American two-stick diamond-shaped kite shares with its Japanese counterparts a flight concept and vague beginnings. The American kite too may be either flat or bowed. In the bowed version, the horizontal stick is bowed, pushing the middle of the kite forward into the wind. This bow acts much the same as the keel of a boat, helping the kite to maintain stability in varying wind currents. It also creates a dihedral angle (a flat V) to the plane of the kite, a stabilizing characteristic the bowed kite shares with airplanes and birds.

The tailless, bowed, two-stick kite as it is known in the West was introduced by an American, William A. Eddy, in the 1890s. His design is a modification of the Malay kite, which is one of the oldest kites in the world. The American version is often called the Eddy/Malay kite. This kite is virtually as wide as it is high, differing in this respect from earlier versions of two-stick kites, which were narrow in proportion to their height and required tails. The older diamond-shaped kites, which go back to the eighteenth century, could be bowed as well, but they lacked the flying stability of Eddy's design.

Of the two types, the bowed kite is the more reliable flyer. A flat kite such as the Nagasaki hata flies with more skittishness. And though it is more difficult to fly, it responds well to sophisticated handling. A bowed kite would be the equivalent of a big car; the flat kite, of a sports car. The giant, as well as the tiny Japanese kite, is a bowed kite, although the average Japanese kite may be flown either flat or bowed.

The structural design of a Japanese kite is determined by flying conditions characteristic of the district in which it is made and flown. The Suruga-dako, Kato told me, is rather fragile so that it cannot be flown at all when there is too much wind. He emphasized that it flies best in the Suruga Bay area in which it is made. The hata kite is made to fly in the Nagasaki district or, altered to a degree imperceptible except to an expert, for flying in another district. Taking this as a clue, the reader's kite should have qualities distinctly suited to its locale and to the flying abilities he wishes it to possess.

The Bones

IF YOU LOOK VERY CAREFULLY at the vertical bones of a Japanese kite, you will notice that they are slightly wider, and therefore heavier, at the top. The weight is gradually increased toward the top by using the bamboo upside down from the way it grows—that is, with the wider base of the tapering bamboo stem at the top. Horizontal bones are also carefully graduated in width and weight with the same effect, the heaviest bones at the top descending to the lightest at the kite's bottom edge. A look at the back of Yanase's beka kite (Plates 34–35) makes this quite clear.

A kite handles better with this weight distribution. This is particularly true of fighting kites, but the beka or any other nonfighter is also meant to handle well in the air. All the movements of a flying kite are made from its top (heavier) edge with the lower (lighter) area following behind. Because the top edge is heavier, it becomes the leading edge and controls the kite's flight.

Kato cautions that the framework of a kite, no matter how complicated or simple, large or small, must be absolutely symmetrical or the kite will not fly straight—"A kite that does not fly straight generally does not fly up," he maintains. He did not wish to share further details about his kite's framework, however, explaining that "my father taught me the Suruga frame technique. This is a secret, and it must remain here. I will not tell it to anyone."

Bamboo is remarkably strong. Part of its strength lies in its flexibility, which allows it to resist breakage by bending with the wind. In the United States, bamboo is commonly available in the form of inexpensive bamboo-slat window blinds. These work well for use in the average small kite. For large kites it is a good idea to consider laminating the thin slats to give them greater strength. Split bamboo lengthwise with a thick-bladed knife, and saw it crosswise with a hack saw. This is the way it is cut in Japan. There, it may be purchased from bamboo yards, the equivalent of Western lumberyards. Experts will have cut the plant out of a bamboo forest at a time when it is strongest and free from insects, and then will have allowed it to dry properly the length of time required for its intended use. In the case of kites, this drying period may be as long as two years. I have used greener bamboo myself, but this meant that my kite was heavier than it would have been had I used properly seasoned stems, and it was not as strong or stable.

Bamboo splits lengthwise easily. It is considerably easier, for instance, than sawing a board by hand along its grain. But bamboo splitting requires practice to make each piece the consistent thickness required. My bamboo supplier could take twenty-foot-tall stems three inches or more in diameter and split them along their length into thinner and thinner strips, ending with strips consistently one-thirty-second of an inch thick. I have not been able to achieve that skill and doubt that I ever will. The beginner has to be satisfied for a while with selecting suitable pieces for his needs out of his best cuttings.

Start by splitting the seasoned bamboo stem in half along its entire length. Line your knife up along one side of the limb notch that is to be found at each node, and with one hand on the handle and the other on the top of the blade, push steadily downward. Make each cut half the former cut until you reach the thickness required.

The Japanese plane, which is pulled toward the user on the cutting stroke, will make narrower sticks out of thick ones (Plate 116). A Western-style plane will do the job as well. Ideas for making simple cutting tools, clamps, measuring devices, and so forth to help make sticks of uniform thickness will occur to you as you work.

The Bridle and Flying Line

THE NUMBER OF LINES comprising the bridle and their length vary greatly from kite to kite. For all kites, the bridle must be exactly in the horizontal center. A rule of thumb for positioning the bridle on the kite's vertical axis is that the tie point, the place where the bridle lines come together and are tied to the kite flying line, is one-third of the way down from the top of the kite. To take into account peculiarities of the kite and the wind, variations in this standard placement are allowed. In a strong wind, move the tie point closer to the top edge, as this will allow the kite to slip through the wind rather than meeting it full against its face. If the wind is light, move the tie point down closer to the kite's vertical center.

The distance measured vertically from the face of the kite to the tie point is one-third to one-half the height of the kite. This measurement, too, varies considerably with a kite's structural design as well as with the flyer's preferences. The Nagasaki kite flyers, for example, set the bridle tie point six feet from the surface of a standard-sized hata fighting kite (about three feet high). By contrast, Indians flying essentially the same kind of fighting kite use one-third the kite's height as their standard. The Indian fighting kite is about two-thirds the size of a hata, but an Indian bridle is, proportionately, considerably shorter.

Giant Japanese kites have extremely long bridles. Most of the standard-sized kites that are flown for fun, such as Kato's Suruga kites, are bridled according to the one-third of the height rule of thumb. Tiny kites also follow this rule. Experimentation, however, is the key to finding your own preference—experimentation and patience.

The strength of the line used for bridles and flying lines (Plates 120–26) must be in proportion to the design and size of the kite. The lines available today are deceptive in their relative strength. A half-inch hemp line may be considerably weaker than an eighth-inch line of fiberglass, plastic, or braided nylon. Whatever its appearance, its strength is defined by its breaking point measured in "pounds pull." Given this information, which generally accompanies purchases of string and rope, a general rule for determining the strength of line required for a particular kite is that it should be three times, in pounds pull, the square feet of the kite's surface.

Japanese kite makers will, when asked, attach the bridles to the kites for a purchaser. This is particularly true of kites using a large number of bridle strings. The Edo kite is a good example. The exact positioning of its many strings is thought to require the expertise of a professional. The Suruga kite bridle, on the other hand, is relatively simple. Accordingly, Kato very seldom attaches a bridle, not because the proper way to position it is absolutely obvious, for it is not, but to allow the owner to feel that the kite exists as a collaboration between himself and the kite maker. "The kite purchaser should put the strings on himself," Kato says. "He will soon learn the correct position, and when he does the kite will have become his own."

Designs and Design Materials

JAPANESE KITE ARTISTS use powdered pigments mixed with water for their kite pictures. Because these dyes bleed rapidly through the paper as they are applied, the picture is first outlined in either *sumi* ink (which does not bleed) or in paraffin wax applied while still in a hot-liquid state. These outlines restrict the pigments to the desired areas (Plate 118).

Kite makers (festival kite makers as well) order paper made especially for their kites. For those who want it, handmade washi similar to the kind they use is available in some countries of the West.

The paste used with washi is commonly available in premixed form throughout Japan. Although it is relatively simple to make, I did not find any kite makers who made their own paste. In the United States this same paste is known simply as wheat flour paste. Since secret techniques and formulas are by no means rare in Japanese traditional crafts, there may very well be special wheat flour pastes being used, although none have come to my attention. Watanabe, the Sanjo kite maker, uses rice in a secret formula to make paste that is waterproof. For aesthetic reasons the thought of modern white glue would at one time have made me wince. Then one day I had to use it; I overcame my distaste and was surprised to find that it produced satisfactory results.

All but the rarest of Westerners would find painting Kabuki or samurai faces impossible. With this in mind, I asked Kato what he thought of plain, unpainted kites. He was horrified. "A kite without a picture is ominous to a Japanese! An unpainted white surface reminds us of a funeral." The traditional idea of reserving white for mourning is changing in Japan, but in any case, kite makers must decide for themselves what to paint—or whether to paint a design at all.

The Tail

A KITE WITH A TAIL, one hears all over Japan, is not a good kite. Instead of a tail, one type of kite has "ears." Because the wind is often gusty in Shizuoka, the Suruga kite is widened a little at the base. These "ears," Kato's term, take the place of a tail. The increased width they lend to the base brings a little additional wind pressure to the bottom of the kite, helping to stabilize it in the same way a tail does.

A good tail, if one is used, should not be heavy. A tail provides more surface area, which reduces the effect of the wind dragging on the kite. A kite that too easily rocks or dives can be stabilized with a good tail. By avoiding a tail altogether, however, your lightweight flying device will remain aloft with less wind. With a tail, it will require more wind, and you will sacrifice maneuverability and response to your handling as well.

Although a tail is not desirable from a Japanese point of view (i.e., they feel that the kite is imperfectly designed), a novice may find one useful, particularly for simple flat kites to be flown in strong winds. You may also feel that the decorative liveliness of a tail adequately compensates for any loss of maneuverability. When a kite has dwindled to a tiny dot far away in the sky, a long tail continues to visibly undulate and dance in a very enjoyable way. The Ceylon cobra kite is ninety-nine percent tail—and a fantastic kite! If you use a tail to help a kite fly, keep in mind that it functions best by offering resistance to the wind, not weight, as is commonly thought.

The Japanese expert readily admits that a very large kite and a very tiny kite, by some paradox, require tails. The giant Hoshubana kite is flown with no tail at all in light winds, but tails are hung from the bottom corners in a strong wind. The Shirone o-dako and the largest Hamamatsu kites are flown with long, sweeping, grass rope tails. Kato's tiny, five-inch-square kites require three tails, each twelve inches long, in order to fly well. Even with tails the little kite tends to spin easily if there is too much wind. It flies best in a wind so gentle and constant as to be barely noticeable on the cheek.

What Kind of Kite Should You Make?

A TINY KITE CAN BE MADE with tissue paper and broomstraws for bones and be flown with the finest sewing thread available. With broomstraws, the balance of the bones should be nearly perfect. The bones on Kato's tiny kite are slivers of bamboo meticulously shaped for balance.

If you base your kite on the modern box kite, similar to Hiroi's box kite, he offers this warning: "Do not make a tapered box kite, one that looks like a wind sock. This is because there is always one best angle of attack for the kite in a given velocity of wind. As a general rule, the faces or wings of the box kite should be the same distance apart from top to bottom, otherwise there will be more than one angle of attack (as with the converging sides of a wind sock), and this will significantly reduce the kite's lift."

In recent times there has been a surge of interest in kites. The new kites that resulted incorporate the twentieth-century knowledge of aerodynamics unknown to earlier kite makers. With the exception of Hiroi's cubic kites, however, the new kites are largely Western developments, and the designers have tended to focus on practical applications rather than aesthetic qualities. Kites with names such as the Rogallo parawing and the Jalbert parafoil have been used by the National Aeronautics and Space Administration for astronaut- and capsule-recovery research. These and other recent kite inventions—the delta wings and the Scott sled, for example—are very exciting kites to fly. All these types are worthy of consideration as a basis for your own kite design.

What kind of kite should you make? I would suggest forgetting the Suruga-dako or any other Japanese kite when it comes to making your own. Suruga-dako for me, and I hope for you, is a kite made in Japan under the sign "Tako Hachi." It is not necessary for us to invent a totally new kite, however; we may instead simply bring something of ourselves to an old kite form. But Western kites, I believe, should derive from Western traditions. If you are unfamiliar with your local traditions, you may establish your own and become the first kite maker of a district, a block, or a house. Myself? I recently discovered that bamboo grows very close to where I have been living in the winter. I'm interested in making, with some help, an 8,000-pound kite, and flying it, also with help, in a mountain field. But what about you? I'd be interested to know what your kite looks like.

FLY IT!

MUCH CAN BE WRITTEN about kite-flying techniques. Let it suffice here to say just a few words. First, flying a kite is easy! Japanese kites fly well because they are carefully made and their Japanese flyers are very careful in their preparations for flying. A Westerner is surprised to see a knowledgeable Japanese kite flyer spending as long as twenty minutes to a half an hour preparing to launch a little kite. During the same time, many Westerners would be trying to jerk their kite skyborne. This is why the less thoughtful flyer's kite, as often as not, is broken and torn in the first few minutes. I must admit that I have frequently fallen into that category. In spite of lapses and ignorance that make me far less than a professional kite flyer, the following comments are aimed at more consistently successful flying. They are drawn from both East and West.

The Wind

LIGHT WINDS ARE BEST for most kites. Unvarying, rather than gusty conditions, are also preferable. A very light breeze, one that is barely noticeable, will fly some very finely designed kites, ones such as the Nagasaki hata and the Suruga kite. A similar breeze, even lighter, is best for tiny kites.

A wind that rustles leaves, and that you can barely feel on your face, is blowing from four to seven miles an hour. A wind moving about twelve miles an hour will keep tree leaves in constant motion. This is the upper limit for average kite flying. If the wind is lifting loose paper off the ground and raising dust, it is too strong for the average kite. If you have been bold enough to build a large kite, a light, steady breeze is still desirable. Very large kites are not house heavy, and hurricane velocities are not necessary for raising them. Kites up to ten feet in height require proportionately less wind and are easier to fly in many ways than smaller kites. Consider also the fact that you generate your own wind: walking and running will produce higher wind velocities on your kite.

Another form of lift occurs for an entirely different reason. The hawks you see soaring languidly around in slow, wide circles, constantly moving upward without beating their wings, are riding bubbles of rising hot air. Such bubbles may be as large as 300 feet in diameter. Fly your kite in one of them and you are flying the "thermals."

Finally, dry winds tend to be gusty, while moisture-laden winds are smooth and unexcelled for kite flying. Kites are traditionally flown in the United States in the early spring, although this is not the best time of year for flying, as the wind tends to blow in gusts. Late summer days are better. In Japan kites are most often flown in January and from early summer to midsummer, the rainy season arriving there in June.

Although kites have been flown in thunderstorms for purposes of weather observation, it is extremely dangerous for the person holding the string or anyone standing nearby. An excellent time for anyone to stop flying kites, Benjamin Franklin notwithstanding, is during an electrical storm. Overhead electric wires should also be avoided as the string will conduct electricity. Although it may be tempting to use a fine wire in lieu of a fiber or plastic line, again, it would be an unwise decision as it would merely increase the danger should it come into contact with a power line. (Incidentally, the overzealous government in 1887 helped reduce drastically the great enthusiasm for kite flying in Japan when it vigorously, too vigorously, emphasized the danger of the country's newly installed electric power lines. I frequently heard this mentioned as an explanation for the decline in kite flying during recent times.) If this danger actually exists, when a kite begins to cross over a power line, the simplest course of action would be to break or let go of the string. I do not believe, however, that with a dry, nonmetallic flying line the flyer is endangered by power lines that are not within his range of vision.

Another safety precaution worth mentioning is a soft cotton glove. I never fail to carry one because I am susceptible to annoying cuts from carelessly handled lines.

Preparations and Launching

OUTSIDE OF STRUCTURAL DESIGN, the main adjustment technique for adapting a kite to wind differences is to move the tie-point position of the bridle up or down, thus changing the kite's angle to the wind. Moving the bridle point up places the leading top edge diagonally into the wind, allowing the kite to almost glide through a stronger wind. Moving the tie point down toward the vertical center puts the kite face at a right angle, which makes the most out of lighter winds.

When making this adjustment be sure each side of the bridle is exactly the same length so that the loop at the tie point is truly at the horizontal dead center. Bridle adjustment is essentially what the cautious Japanese flyer is doing in the fifteen or twenty minutes before he actually lifts his kite into the air. More surprising to the Westerner, perhaps, is that he is also calming himself for a controlled, even liftoff, as opposed to girding himself for a sudden blastoff.

At one end of the launching procedure spectrum is the already mentioned method devised by Hiroi, who taught himself to fly kites from a fixed, stationary position on the sloping roof of his house. The Nagasaki hata kite is thrown like a model glider with the wind, then abruptly pulled back for lift. Both of these stationary launches are difficult.

At the opposite end of the spectrum is running with a lot of line out. If there is no wind and you have the energy to run a long time, your kite will stay up for as long as you keep jogging. This is good exercise, but it is most difficult to control a kite while running. For that reason it is the least satisfactory way of launching a kite. I would recommend running only as a last resort, and then only if the wind is rustling the leaves at treetop level and you think you will be able to get your kite up to that height by running. As often as not, I have found that treetop wind is quite elusive. A few minutes after I start running, it stops blowing. Anyway, there are several much better ways to get your kite up.

A compromise between running and letting the kite lift right out of your fingers is to let out fifty to one hundred feet of string along the ground with a friend holding the kite up at the opposite end. On your signal, he gives it a gentle, even boost upward, and you pull evenly back on your string. The long line will give the kite enough leeway to adjust its balance in its first seconds of flight. Use a shorter length of string for slight winds, a longer one for stronger winds to protect it from diving and crashing.

Updrafts form on the windward side of hills, buildings, and groups of trees. These are ideal places for starting a kite upward. They are the best substitute for running in otherwise becalmed air. Stand just below the crest of the hill for best results. The opposite, or leeward, side of a hill should be avoided, for there, perhaps just above your head, where you cannot feel it, is a downdraft through which kites simply cannot pass.

In the Air

ONCE THE KITE IS FLYING, to keep it up the simple rule of thumb is: pull down sharply and repeatedly on the string if the kite begins to fall and let the string out as long as the kite continues to move away into the sky. Alternately letting out more string and pulling in a smaller amount than you've let out will coax a kite to a point in the sky where its lift is equalized and it will continue to float. Your kite will not climb past this point. Should you continue to let out string it will move longitudinally farther away from you. In this case, due to the added weight of the string, the kite will be pulled slightly lower.

A kite automatically assumes its own zenith. It is difficult if not impossible to alter this position. However, it may be of some use to try getting your kite more directly overhead by letting the string out while at the same time running toward the kite. Western kite flyers when striving for altitude records fly box kites in tandem, a method that helps to lift the weight of the string as well as increase the string angle at each point of connection.

The tendency in Western kite flying has generally been toward gaining greater stability and altitude. Should you wish, however, to move your kite at will through the sky, as do the Nagasaki hata fighters, it may be accomplished in the following manner. First, though, keep in mind that the flat kite that darts and skips seemingly uncontrollably is the one with which the greatest control is possible. When the kite is momentarily in a stabilized position near its zenith, suddenly let out two to three feet of string. The kite will then start to circle. When the uppermost leading edge approaches the direction you want the kite to move in, pull the string in evenly toward you at a moderate speed. If the leading edge was pointed left, the kite will go left, and vice versa. Note that your kite will do this only if it has some of the characteristics of the flat hata or is designed with the weight increasing slightly toward the top. Mastery of this flying technique will make you the master of your kite in the sky. It is not an easily acquired skill, but endless fun to pursue.

While living in Japan, I made trips through Southeast Asia. In Ceylon (now Sri Lanka), I visited a kite maker who taught me some of the subtleties of kite flying. He coaxed a kite upward for me by jackknifing his control hand straight back to his shoulder, the elbow held at a ninety-degree angle to the ground. This tugging motion was given a smoothness and precision not possible when the string is pulled sideways, the way most kite flyers seem naturally to pull it. He next sent up a very light kite, one slightly more fragile looking than the first, and handed me the string. When I asked if the jackknife tugging technique was okay for this kite, he said no, and showed me what to do. "For this one you must pull the string with only your forefinger," he explained, while demonstrating a "come here" gesture.

The session with the Ceylonese master ascertained what I had long suspected: ordinary kite flying is easy, but there are also techniques for gaining advanced mastery that require remarkably subtle skills.

If available, a professional's help is invaluable. But these are rare birds indeed. Not rare at all are kite-loving children who, while practiced, are usually insufficiently articulate. If a child can't tell you how, he may be able to show you how. Finally, if nothing you do gets your kite up into the sky, it may be that it is simply the wrong type for the locale or the existing wind conditions. In that case, stop trying, before your frustration turns to anger and the kite is broken. Try getting on a bicycle to enjoy the feel of the wind on your face instead of in your hand. Then look around for other kinds of kites. The best place to look, of course, is in the sky.

One day in Japan I spotted one of Kato's Suruga kites flying high above Shizuoka. I drove toward it and when I was close enough to see the string I got out of the car and walked over to the owner. As is often the case anywhere in the world, this kite flyer was a middle-aged man. He wore a subdued black and gray kimono. A small child was at his side, craning his head upward toward the kite. As it may be that the devil is only a fallen angel, the adult may only be a fallen child. I imagined that the first soldier to fly a Suruga kite over his master's castle wall in this same area three hundred years ago as a symbol of victory must have taken the victory kite from the hand of a small child. Although kites are flown by adults and children, the person holding the string is, in a sense, always a child.

Tatsusaburo Kato lamented the decline of childhood in contemporary Japanese society. He sadly observed, "Children in former days were quite childlike. For instance, most of the boys wished to grow up to be generals—without thinking much about the life of a general. Winter games for children were kite flying, top spinning, and bouncing balls, and these occupied them all day long. Children today are asked to study so hard that they don't have any time for play. Even our kindergarteners bring home large amounts of homework. These poor children! I wish they could study hard, be obedient—and play childish games." His eyes sparkled with the thought of innocent pleasures. Perhaps that is why we must fly kites late into life.

EPILOGUE

I ACCIDENTALLY STUMBLED ONTO TINY KITES, ironically enough, after I had returned to the United States. Soon after my return I met Fumio Yoshimura, a sculptor who also makes kites. "The tiny ones," he told me, "are the size of the nail of my little finger. I fly them over the rising hot air of a charcoal brazier with a flying line of human hair." These may be the smallest kites we will ever see.

In Japan I had found some that were slightly smaller than a postage stamp. They contrasted strangely with the giants I admired and made myself.

I flew my own large kites quite often on a sand beach of Suruga Bay. My wife held the big kites aloft while I braced myself holding a line a hundred feet down the beach and waited for a slight advantage in the wind. At the right moment I imagined I would run at breakneck speed to pull the kite airborne. But when I began running and the full force of the wind hit the face of my large kite, it was as if I were trying to run in sand up to my knees. The drag was enormous as the kite went up. The feeling was like trying to fly a ponderous anchor at the end of a long rope.

The tiny kites I acquired (Plates 128–30) offered a more relaxed kind of pleasure. Between my appearances at the beach, which attracted crowds of curious Japanese, I enjoyed the delights of a small kite. Sitting comfortably on the tatami mats of my home, with my legs stretched out full length while leaning back on my elbows, I would direct the wind of a fan so it blew softly over my shoulder, the light breeze pushing against a tiny kite dipping and turning in the far corner of the room at the end of a short thread.

A friend said, "Not so exciting." To which I replied, "When it crashes it doesn't sound like the big ones, but the feeling to me is the same. When an ant dies, it is as dead as a bear, and its dying causes it as much pain."

A tiny kite alive in the air has a wonderful personality. As I watch one float around like an exploring butterfly, I can feel the tensions in my face relax into a smile.

In my search for the tiniest kite I traveled outside Japan, throughout Southeast Asia. I visited kite makers who make such beautiful kites and live in such utter poverty that either aspect could bring tears to the eyes. During these travels I heard of yet another kite, one that I invite you to search for with me. This is the famous but extraordinarily long and rare centipede (in Japanese, *mukade*) kite. The kite is made of many small paper and bamboo discs tied loosely together at regular intervals. In flight, the wind separates each of the discs, creating a long centipede or snakelike form.

I was frequently asked if I had ever seen the long centipede kites. I usually answered that the longest kite I had ever seen was Tsutomu Hiroi's 300-foot mammoth which he modeled on a Chinese one (Plate 127), something really unbelievable to see flying in the sky. "No, that's not what I mean," my informant would respond. "These centipede kites are 750 feet long! I have not seen them myself, but I'm told they exist."

Can you imagine this incredible kite, a 750-foot-long paper serpent writhing through the sky? I was told about this kite by several very reliable people. I am sure it exists. But where? We shall have to begin our search for this kite in China.

A SELECT READING LIST

THIS LIST INCLUDES BOOKS on Japan that I have enjoyed. It covers a wide range of subjects that will help bring to life old and new Japan. I offer it in the hope that it will bring pleasure to other readers as well.

Austin, Robert; Ueda, Koichiro; and Levy, Dana. *Bamboo*. New York and Tokyo: Walker/Weatherhill, 1970.

Basho. *The Narrow Road to the Deep North and Other Travel Sketches*. N. Yuasa (tr.). Harmondsworth, England: Penguin, 1972.

Blyth, R. H. *Haiku: Eastern Culture, Spring, Summer–Autumn, Autumn–Winter*. 4 vols. Tokyo: Hokuseido, 1949–52.

————. *Zen in English Literature and Oriental Classics*. Tokyo: Hokuseido, 1970.

Bownas, Geoffrey. *Japanese Rainmaking and Other Folk Practices*. London: Allen & Unwin, 1963.

Brummit, Wyatt. *Kites*. New York: Golden Press, Western Publishing, 1971.

Busch, Noel F. *The Horizon Concise History of Japan*. New York: American Heritage, 1972.

Castile, Rand. *The Way of Tea*. New York and Tokyo: Weatherhill, 1971.

Choe, Sang-su. *The Survey of Korean Kites*. Seoul: Korean Information Service, 1958.

Culin, Stuart. *Games of the Orient: Korea, China, Japan*. First pub. 1895. Tokyo and Rutland, Vt.: Tuttle, 1958.

Dunn, Charles J. *Everyday Life in Traditional Japan*. New York: Putnam, 1969.

Engel, Heinrich. *The Japanese House: A Tradition for Contemporary Architecture*. Tokyo and Rutland, Vt.: Tuttle, 1964.

Hart, Clive. *Kites: An Historical Survey*. New York: Praeger, 1967.

————. *Your Book of Kites*. London: Faber & Faber, 1964.

Hearn, Lafcadio. *Glimpses of Unfamiliar Japan*. First pub. 1900. Tokyo and Rutland, Vt.: Tuttle, 1969.

Henderson, Harold G. *An Introduction to Haiku*. Garden City, N.Y.: Doubleday Anchor, 1958.

Herrigel, Eugen. *Zen in the Art of Archery*. New York: Random House, 1971.

Hiroi, Tsutomu. *Tako* (Kites). Tokyo: Mainichi Newspapers, 1973.

———. *Tako* (Kites) in the series *Tanoshii Zokei* (Fun with Making Things). Tokyo: Bijutsu Shuppan-sha, 1969.

———. *Tako: Sora no Zokei* (Kites: Art in the Air). Tokyo: Bijutsu Shuppan-sha, 1972.

Ienaga, Saburo. *History of Japan*. Tokyo: Japan Travel Bureau, 1969.

Itoh, Teiji. *Traditional Domestic Architecture of Japan*. R. L. Gage (tr.). New York and Tokyo: Weatherhill/Heibonsha, 1972.

Jippensha, Ikku. *Shank's Mare*. First pub. 1802–22 as *Hizakurige*. Tokyo and Rutland, Vt.: Tuttle, 1971.

Jue, David F. *Chinese Kites*. Tokyo and Rutland, Vt.: Tuttle, 1971.

Kaemmerer, Eric. A. *Trades and Crafts of Old Japan*. Tokyo and Rutland Vt.: Tuttle, 1961.

Kato, Shuichi. *Form, Style, Tradition: Reflections of Japanese Art and Society*. J. Bester (tr.). Berkeley: University of California Press, 1971.

Kawabata, Yasunari. *Snow Country*. E. G. Seidensticker (tr.). New York: Knopf, 1969.

Keene, Donald. *Living Japan*. Garden City, N.Y.: Doubleday, 1959.

Kirkup, James. *Japan Behind the Fan*. London: Dent, 1970.

Kuck, Loraine. *The World of the Japanese Garden*. New York and Tokyo: Walker/Weatherhill, 1968.

Kung, David S. "Japanese Kites: A Vanishing Art." Unpublished manuscript, University of Hawaii Library Archives.

Leach, Bernard. *A Potter in Japan*. London: Faber & Faber, 1960.

Mishima, Yukio. *The Temple of the Golden Pavilion*. I. Morris (tr.). New York: Knopf, 1959.

Morse, Edward S. *Japanese Homes and Their Surroundings*. First pub. 1900. New York: Dover, 1961.

Munsterberg, Hugo. *The Arts of Japan*. Tokyo and Rutland, Vt.: Tuttle, 1958.

Natsume, Soseki. *Botchan*. U. Sasaki (tr.). Tokyo and Rutland, Vt.: Tuttle, 1967.

Newman, Alex R., and Ryerson, Egerton. *Japanese Art: A Collectors' Guide*. London: Bell, 1964.

Oka, Hideyuki, and Sakai, Michikazu. *How to Wrap Five Eggs*. New York: Harper & Row, 1967.

Okakura, Kakuzo. *The Book of Tea*. First pub. 1906. New York: Dover, 1967.

Phelan, Nancy. *Pillow of Grass*. London: Macmillan, 1969.

Piggot, Juliet. *Japanese Mythology*. London and New York: Hamlyn, 1973.

Pomeroy, Charles A. *Traditional Crafts of Japan*. New York and Tokyo: Walker/Weatherhill, 1967.

Richie, Donald. *The Inland Sea*. New York and Tokyo: Weatherhill, 1971.

Rokujiuyen. *The Magical Carpenter of Japan*. F. V. Dickins (tr.). Tokyo and Rutland, Vt.: Tuttle, 1965.

Saito, Tadao. *High Fliers: Colorful Kites from Japan*. San Francisco: Japan Publications, 1969.

———. *Tako no Katachi* (The Shapes of Kites). Tokyo: Iwasaki Bijutsu-sha, 1971.

Sato, Koji, and Kuzunishi, Sosei. *The Zen Life*. R. Victoria (tr.). New York, Tokyo, and Kyoto: Weatherhill/Tankosha, 1972.

Seki, Keigo, and Adams, Robert. *Folk Tales of Japan*. Chicago: University of Chicago Press, 1962.

Statler, Oliver. *Japanese Inn*. New York: Random House, 1961.

Sugimura, Tsune, and Kasai, Shigeo. *Hachijo: Isle of Exile*. New York and Tokyo: Weatherhill, 1973.

Sugimura, Tsune, and Ogawa, Masataka. *The Enduring Crafts of Japan*. New York and Tokyo: Walker/ Weatherhill, 1968.

Suzuki, Isami. *Itome-tsuke Hiden* (How to Fix Bridle Strings: The Secrets). Hamamatsu: Hamamatsu Kite Association.

Suzuki, Shunryu. *Zen Mind, Beginner's Mind*. New York and Tokyo: Walker/Weatherhill, 1970.

Tawara, Yusaku, and Sonobe, Kiyoshi. *Nihon no Tako* (Japanese Kites). Tokyo: Kikkasha, 1970.

Toland, John. *The Rising Sun*. New York: Random House, 1970.

Wagenvoord, James. *Flying Kites in Fun, Art, and War*. New York: Macmillan, 1968.

Warner, Langdon. *The Enduring Art of Japan*. New York: Grove, 1958.

Watanabe, Kurasuke. *Nagasaki Hata Ko* (A Study of Nagasaki Hata Kites). Nagasaki: Folk Arts Society of Nagasaki Prefecture, 1959.

Yanagi, Soetsu. *Folk-Crafts in Japan*. Tokyo: Kokusai Bunka Shinkokai (Society for International Cultural Relations), 1956.

Yee, Chiang. *The Silent Traveller in Japan*. New York: Norton, 1972.

Yolen, Jane. *World on a String: The Story of Kites*. Cleveland: World, 1969.

ABOUT THE AUTHOR

TAL STREETER WAS BORN in Oklahoma City in 1934 and graduated from the University of Kansas, after which he moved to New York City to work as a sculptor. He has held positions at Dartmouth College and the University of North Carolina as artist-in-residence. At present he teaches at the School of Arts, State University of New York, College at Purchase, where he is in the Division of Visual Arts and responsible for three-dimensional design. He makes his home in Millbrook, New York, with his wife and daughter. Best known as a sculptor of lean, modern works in steel, he exhibits regularly in the United States and Japan and his sculpture is represented in many art museums and other public collections.

As a writer, Mr. Streeter's articles have appeared frequently in art and architecture journals. He has traveled widely in East Asia and lived both in Korea, where he was Fulbright professor and was commissioned to make one of Korea's largest contemporary sculptures, and in Japan. It was during his Japan stay that he turned his attention seriously to writing, photography, and the construction of large paper and bamboo kites employing modern idioms within a framework of traditional Japanese materials and techniques. The present book is one of the happy results of this unusual exploration.

The "weathermark" identifies this books as a publication
of John Weatherhill, Inc., publishers of fine books on
Asia and the Pacific. Editors in charge, Ronald V. Bell,
Nina Raj. Book design, typography, and layout of illustrations,
Dana Levy. Production supervision, Mitsuo Okado. Com-
position, General Printing Company, Yokohama. Engraving,
Nissha, Kyoto. Printing, General Printing Company and
Nissha. Binding, Makoto Binderies, Tokyo. The type of the
main text is in set 12-point Monotype Perpetua with hand-set
14- and 18-point Perpetua Light Titling for display.